M000103513

Weddings

The Magic of Creating Your Own Ceremony

The first duty of love is to listen.

—Paul Tillich

Weddings

The Magic of Creating Your Own Ceremony

Henry S. Basayne
and
Linda R. Janowitz, Ph.D.

BookPartners
Wilsonville, Oregon

Copyright © 1999 by Henry S. Basayne and Linda R. Janowitz
All rights reserved
Printed in U.S.A.
ISBN 1-885221-92-4

Portions of this book were originally published as *Let Us Make a Wedding: A Guidebook for Creating Your Own Ceremony*, Copyright © 1992 by Henry S. Basayne and Linda R. Janowitz, and as *It's Your Wedding: A Workbook for Creating Your Own Ceremony*, Copyright © 1981 by Linda R. Janowitz and Henry S. Basayne. This version is completely revised, enlarged and updated.

Copyright permissions will be found at the end of the book.

                    Library of Congress Cataloging-in-Publication Data
Basayne, Henry S., 1927–
    Weddings : the magic of creating your own ceremony / Henry S.
Basayne and Linda R. Janowitz.
        p.   cm.
    Includes bibliographical references and index.
    ISBN 1-885221-92-4 (paper)
    1. Marriage service. 2. Marriage customs and rites. 3. Weddings.
I. Janowitz, Linda R., 1941–   II. Title.
HQ745.B378   1999
392'.5--dc21   99-23465
                                                                    CIP

Cover design by Richard Ferguson
Text design by Sheryl Mehary
Illustrations by Margaret Foley

No part of this book may be used or reproduced in any manner whatsoever without prior written permission except in the case of brief quotations embodied in critical articles and reviews.
For information contact:

                    BookPartners, Inc.
                        P. O. Box 922
                Wilsonville, Oregon 97071

To the hundreds of couples
whose imagination, creativity
and love for each other
expanded our horizons,
we express our deep affection and appreciation.

To Donald A. Linden
whose encouragement, support,
levelheadedness, and prodding
enabled us to finish this book,
we offer our enduring love and thanks.

Contents

Chapter 1

Why Write Your Own Wedding Ceremony?

A successful marriage requires falling in
love many times, always with the same person.
—Mignon McLaughlin

History and Hollywood have taught us to think of wedding ceremonies as beginning with "Dearly beloved...," continuing with the "Do you...Do you's..." and winding up with "I now pronounce you...." Safe, comfortable, and traditional—but rarely reflecting anything unique about the couple, their commitment, their love, or their view of what makes their marriage special.

Many couples now choose ceremonies that celebrate their own values and personalities, their own special circumstances, and their own commitments. There are numerous motivations for creating personal weddings, such as different ethnic or religious backgrounds, a second marriage, children from previous relationships, or a desire to honor your own philosophical, political, or social beliefs.

For many couples, the traditional religious wedding is exactly what they want. After all, traditional weddings have served generations of brides and grooms—and served them well. Tradition offers the comfort, familiarity, and continuity that hold communities together. Couples who are comfortable within their established religion will look there for the formalization of their wedding vows. However, even within the most conservative religions, spiritual leaders may encourage the couple to personalize their vows.

For other couples, though, a traditional wedding ceremony just doesn't fit. Merely altering a standard wedding ceremony around the edges won't do. They may have philosophical differences with traditional religions and yet find civil ceremonies too sterile. Some may not fit into traditional religious frameworks: nontheists; agnostics; those who do not belong to a congregation; those who reject the premarital requirements of their church, synagogue, or mosque; those who are marrying someone of another faith or ethnic background; those who seek a same-sex ceremony of commitment. These couples may be happier and more at ease creating a ceremony that matches their life circumstances and celebrates the uniqueness of their marriage.

Couples who have thought deeply about the relationship they intend to create want the ceremony to express those thoughts. They may wish to give voice to their strongly held beliefs. Or they may find challenge and satisfaction in creating a ceremony that reflects their lives. Even when it bears the stamp of a couple's originality and departs from the tried and true, the ceremony can retain its sacred importance and meaning.

Some couples may want to share with their wedding guests their thoughts on important issues, or their dreams, goals, and commitments. One couple wanted to find a way to honor the memory of a recently deceased parent. Another couple, leaving immediately after the wedding for the Peace Corps, wanted the ceremony to include their belief in personal social action.

Whether it is a couple remarrying after a divorce, a bride and groom who have been living together for a number of years, an older married couple renewing their vows, a gay or lesbian couple creating a ceremony of commitment, or a couple coming to the altar with the bride seven months pregnant—each pair has the need for a ceremony that reflects their distinctiveness.

ॐ ॐ ॐ

Why the Wedding Ceremony Is So Important

Throughout history, rites of passage have played a major role in creating and maintaining community. Rituals that commemorate births, marriages, deaths and other important life events are vital links that draw people together and create community.

Rituals separate extraordinary moments and life-changing events from the ordinary affairs of everyday life. They mark profoundly significant life transitions. They bring the community together to witness events and cement relationships. They strengthen the social network and remind people of the necessity of supporting each other.

Through most of history, participants in these rites haven't had much say in *how* these ceremonies are celebrated. Only in recent times, and in select societies, have we enjoyed the freedom to customize our rites of passage. This freedom of choice to make our ceremonies personal and meaningful is a gift we now can give to each other and to those who love and support us.

So here you are, about to celebrate a momentous and joyous ritual that marks the start of your new life together. What does this celebration mean to you? Is your focus on the party, the music, flowers, cake, and photographs? Or will you choose to dedicate a significant amount of your time and energy to emphasizing your relationship and the important foundations you are building for your life together? Your answers to these and other questions in this book are the first steps toward creating a wedding ceremony that is personal and authentic.

ॐ ॐ ॐ

The Meaning and Significance of the Wedding Vows

Vows are the essence—the heart and soul—of every wedding ceremony. They are the expression of the couple's promises and commitments to each other and to society—the fundamental purpose of the ceremony.

It is impossible to overstate the importance of the wedding vows. You should view these promises as the core of your marriage. In times of difficulty, returning to your vows will enable you to renew your faith in each other and in your marriage. Use these promises as the source of strength that allows you to work through difficult times.

Although in the 1960s and 1970s it was fashionable to promise to remain together "as long as love shall last," it is now apparent that long, healthy, and satisfying marriages need a much stronger commitment. The rate of divorce in our society proves how difficult it is to maintain a successful relationship. Marriage requires a deep commitment to love and cherish each other, to accept differences and to work together to resolve problems. Couples with weaker commitments to marriage are far less likely to survive the difficulties that lie ahead.

Writing your own wedding vows creates a fundamental building block for your relationship. It is a life-enhancing way for each of you to look within yourself, to find the source of your own strength and devotion, and to articulate the promises that will enable you to travel successfully on your journey together, through thick and thin, through sickness and health, through riches and poverty.

Making promises that you yourself have created is a powerful statement to each other and to your friends, your family, your community, and your deity. Declaring your vows publicly emphasizes their importance, and reminds those who hear you to support you in keeping your word. This public statement to your own community helps nurture strong, durable, and loving relationships.

In creating your promises, you may find that traditional vows express what you want to say, and that's fine. But if the time-honored words don't fit, you will want to write your own.

You may be most comfortable writing your vows together and saying identical words. Or each of you may have your own slant on what you want to promise, and your vows will be quite different. The important thing is that your promises are authentic, and that you both understand what you are promising each other.

ॐ ॐ ॐ

Writing Your Own Wedding Ceremony Can Create a Stronger Marriage

One of the special advantages of building a wedding ceremony together is the wonderful opportunity to talk, to explore, and to learn more about each other. You will discover that this process reveals hidden facets of your personalities: dreams, experiences, uncertainties, personality differences, and unspoken expectations. This joint effort is a marvelous chance to see how well you work together. As you go along, notice how you communicate, negotiate, compromise, or struggle for control; how you divide labor, cope with stress, and make room for each other.

The act of developing a personal ceremony has value and meaning beyond the ceremony itself. It will encourage you, as a couple, to consider your relationship, and to find out what's important to you and your partner as you share, question, and jointly take the first step in your married life. The process adds meaning and depth to your relationship. It reminds you that, in addition to being a couple, you are also unique and separate individuals. It heightens your awareness of your attitudes and beliefs, and helps you articulate your values to each other. It can lead you to a wedding that expresses pleasure, delight, and excitement, as well as profound meaning.

As unexpected differences arise, for some couples the process becomes an acid test of their relationship. But for most it will be a thrilling adventure, resulting in better understanding, mutual respect, warmth, and intimacy.

Your shared goals, values, and expectations form the basis of your wedding ceremony. The more open you are with each other, and the more you share yourself, the more likely you are to enter marriage with a strong foundation of mutual respect, admiration, and acceptance.

According to John M. Gottman, Ph.D., the first requirement for a strong, healthy marriage is a keen sense that you fully know each other—that each of you has a *love map* of your partner's inner life.

Dr. Gottman, the author of *The Seven Principles for Making Marriage Work* is a research psychologist who has studied married couples for decades. He teaches that the second requirement is to have a profound sense of fondness and admiration for each other. Only when these two conditions are met can couples turn toward each other and find workable solutions to their problems.

Working together on your wedding ceremony lets you see each other in a deep and intimate way. It may not be easy, but we recommend that you push through your barriers of self-restraint, open yourselves to each other, share your differences as well as your similarities, and explore your dreams.

ॐ ॐ ॐ

How to Use This Book

Our purpose is to show you creative options that go beyond the familiar and the routine, and express the meaning of your relationship in your own wedding ceremony. We want to stimulate your thinking and encourage you to design a rite of passage that will make your wedding the most enjoyable and memorable day that it can be.

This is a book to be *done,* not merely to be read. We offer a wide range of possibilities, a spectrum of examples, and guidelines for organizing the ceremony.

Your wedding belongs to you alone. You will make your own promises or vows, decide how long your ceremony will take, include as many people as you want in your wedding party, and choose to have or do without a maid of honor or best man. Your ceremony can be held at any time and any place that you both decide. You can release live doves or reenact ancient traditions. You can invent new rituals that capture the essence of what makes this wedding yours. You can select some guests for special roles in the ceremony, or have all the guests participate with candle-lighting, bouquet-building, or responsive readings. The celebrant can perform the whole ceremony, none of it, or something in between.

Remember, your wedding is *your* event—yours to shape exactly as you want. Stretch the customary boundaries until the ceremony expresses precisely what you intend and reflects your uniqueness as a couple.

ৡৡৡৡৡ

One half of me is yours, the other half yours—
Mine own, I would say; but if mine, then yours,
And so all yours!

—William Shakespeare

Chapter 2

Setting the Tone

Joy, gentle friends! Joy and fresh days of love
Accompany your hearts!

—William Shakespeare

Get your notebook and take a deep breath. You are about to start the exciting, creative, and sometimes frustrating adventure of creating the wedding ceremony of your dreams! Here are a few things you should know up front.

First, there are significant legal aspects to the wedding ceremony. You are making a contract with each other. It's a contract about rights and responsibilities, money, property, children, and inheritances, among other things. Because you are creating a contract, the state has a stake in making sure that the contract is clear, legal, and binding. The wedding ceremony, therefore, must include an explicit declaration that you each agree to marry the other. As long as you make that declaration in some manner during the ceremony, the rest is a matter of choice or tradition.

Second, we would like you to understand *our* point of view. We believe that the process of creating your own wedding ceremony can be a significant step in building the foundation of your relationship. The more energy you are willing to invest in the process, the more you will learn about each other and about the ways in which you relate to each other. In this book you will find questions designed to encourage the two of you to share who you are, how you think, and what you want. These questions are not limited to information about the wedding ceremony or the reception, but touch on your philosophy, values, and dreams.

Third, we want to make clear the importance of focusing on your differences as well as your similarities. The ability to discuss, understand, negotiate, and accept differences is one of the critical skills couples need in order to successfully maintain a long-term relationship. We have also found that *differences* inspire creativity. We encourage you to negotiate your differences, find creative alternatives (not always compromises) that meet the needs of both of you, and acknowledge some of those differences in your ceremony. Finding ways to meet your partner's needs puts you on the path toward a happy marriage.

We draw a sharp distinction between the wedding ceremony— the heart of the event—and the wedding reception—the celebration. This book is primarily about your wedding ceremony. In this chapter you will find a number of questions that will help you think about this ritual—about the what, when, where, why, and how issues. Our goal is to have you think, talk, and go beyond your pre-set notions. Other questions are about you—your dreams, values, and beliefs; your relationship; the pressures you may feel; and the obstacles you have before you. Take our questions as a starting point and then add your own questions and answers.

Be sure to take notes of your memories, ideas, words, and images. These will become the building blocks for your own special ceremony.

ॐ ॐ ॐ

Your Dream Wedding

The first four questions have to do with the kind of wedding you want and how you want to feel when the ceremony is over. These questions provide a foundation for making other important decisions. The tone you choose will influence every detail of your wedding, including the setting, clothing, music, and especially the language you use in the ceremony.

1. ***What would your dream wedding be like? What was the loveliest, most meaningful wedding you ever attended?***

    It's not unusual for one of you to have more vivid wedding fantasies than the other. Express your ideal vision without regard for life's mundane realities, such as your budget. Take your time. Helping each other to daydream is a delightful way to feel closer. Take care not to lapse into feeling guilty or sad because you can't fulfill your partner's desires or your own. Sharing the dream is what's more important at this point. And sometimes you can find creative ways to incorporate at least some elements of your ideal wedding into your real wedding.

2. ***What kind of wedding are you actually going to create?***

    Keep in mind what you shared during your time of daydreaming, but now bring reality into the discussion and talk about what you think is possible.

    *   Do you want your ceremony to be a tradition-filled ritual, a festive pageant, an intimate time of sharing, an ethnic experience, a contemporary celebration, or…?
    *   Will your reception be a simple picnic in a beautiful park, a small gathering of close friends in your backyard, a cocktail party in a local restaurant, a gala event in a hotel ballroom, a festive dinner party in a friend's home, an outdoor wedding overlooking the sea, or…?

3. ***What mood do you want to create with your ceremony?***

    *   How do you want to feel when the ceremony is over? Joyful, intimate, serious, solemn, poignant, warm, profound, committed, relaxed, relieved, triumphant, or…?

4. *What limitations do you have to consider in your planning?*

   • What is your budget for the wedding? How will your pocketbook affect the ceremony, the reception, and the other accoutrements of the wedding?
   • Will your site or the time of year affect the kind of ceremony you create—limited space, a remote location, difficult access, or bad weather?
   • Do you or your guests have any disabilities or special needs that require accommodation?

ॐ ॐ ॐ

Determine Your Preferences

The next five questions focus on the ceremony itself—the heart of this life-changing event. You are creating a rite of passage to mark the start of a new phase in your life. These questions will help you think about what is most important to you and how your ceremony will reflect your values and priorities.

1. *What do you want your vows and the ceremony to signify?*

   • Are you acknowledging the existence of a commitment that you two have already made?
   • Are you sharing with others the beginning of this new phase in your relationship?
   • Are you voicing a commitment that will substantially change your current relationship?
   • Or...?

2. *How traditional or non-traditional, religious or non-religious, do you want your wedding to be? How important are family or ethnic customs? Do you want—*

   • A traditional religious ceremony with personal vows?

- A ceremony free of religious overtones but with abundant ritual?
- A contemporary ceremony with a traditional tone?
- A ceremony rich in ethnic customs?
- An intimately personal ceremony?
- A spiritual ceremony with personal meaning?
- Or...?

3. *Will the ceremony truly represent you, or are you concerned with meeting the expectations of parents, relatives or friends?*

- If you are feeling pressure from others, what would you have to do to satisfy them?
- Can you find creative ways to meet the needs of others without compromising your own?
- Remember, this is *your* wedding, and to be meaningful it is important that it expresses who you are. Try to accommodate the desires of other people, but not at the expense of giving up the wedding you want and deserve. We'll have more tips on how to do this later.

4. *Do you prefer long ceremonies or short, informal ones?*

- A minimal ceremony can take just a minute or so if all you want are the standard vows. But this approach may leave your guests wondering if something important really happened.
- An average ceremony takes fifteen to thirty minutes and allows plenty of time for poetry, music, and rituals.
- A long ceremony may take an hour or more and may involve extensive ritual and tradition, and plenty of opportunity to present an elaborate and creative production.
- In thinking about the length of the ceremony, take into consideration your guests' ages and physical limitations, whether they will be standing or sitting, and what the weather may be like. The setting of the wedding, indoors or out, large hall or small, are factors that influence how easy it will be to hear your voices.

5. *How much of the ceremony would you like to create yourselves?*

- Create the whole ceremony from scratch to express exactly what you want.
- Choose bits and pieces from the ceremonies in this or other books and put them together to express your feelings.
- In a traditional ceremony, write your own vows, and consider adding special poetry or music.
- Work with a celebrant who will listen to your needs and then do most of the writing for you.
- Or...?
- Don't limit yourself by anxiety or feelings of inadequacy. We'll provide all the structure you need to do it exactly the way you want.

ॐ ॐ ॐ

More Choices and Decisions

The following questions will get you started thinking about a few more specific aspects of the wedding ceremony and celebration.

1. *When and where will you hold your wedding?*

Setting the date and choosing the wedding site are the first two steps. Unless you plan to hold your wedding in your home or the home of a friend, you will probably find that many desirable settings are reserved far in advance, sometimes as much as a year ahead. Visiting prospective sites, choosing one, and negotiating the fee begin to add a concrete sense of reality to your wedding plans. Knowing the location of the ceremony and reception will help you visualize the kind of wedding you want.

- What time of year do you want to be married—winter, summer, spring, or fall? Will you choose a date of significance or one of convenience? Consider what it will mean to have your anniversary at this time every year.

- What about selecting a holiday, such as New Year's Eve or Day, Valentine's Day, Independence Day, Labor Day, Thanksgiving, or Christmas? Or some other holiday, when you can enjoy a long weekend? If you do choose a holiday, you might want to incorporate its symbolism into the ceremony.
- What about time of day—morning, afternoon, or evening? Sunrise, sunset, midnight, or noon—each adds a particular flavor.
- Will you choose a place that has sentimental or symbolic meaning for you?
- Will it be indoors or outdoors? Will you need a bad-weather alternative?
- An outdoor wedding might take place in a park, a historic site, a garden or mountaintop, the beach, or a circle of trees in the forest.
- You can hold an indoor wedding in a home, a hall, a church or chapel, a restaurant, a private club, an art gallery or museum, a historic mansion or other building.
- The site you choose can represent a special interest you share, the place you met, or a location that will inspire you and your guests.
- If you have more than about seventy-five guests, or your ceremony takes place outdoors where there may be environmental noise, consider the use of a microphone and amplification. With a public address system (often provided by the site or a disc jockey) you and the celebrant can maintain an intimate or conversational tone and still be heard by guests in back.

2. Who will officiate at your wedding?

- Will your celebrant be a cooperative rabbi, priest, or minister, a justice of the peace, judge, Humanist Counselor, ship's captain, or some other functionary who can legally perform the ceremony?

- Do you both like the celebrant? Do you feel there's compatibility, that he or she listens to you and is willing and able to meet your needs? Is there a sense of comfort and openness in talking?
- Will the celebrant allow you to write the entire ceremony, only the vows, or nothing at all?
- If the celebrant plans to write all or part of the ceremony, will he or she agree to let you read and edit it?
- Is the celebrant willing to meet with you at least twice to develop the ceremony, in addition to attending the rehearsal?
- Because your wedding is so important to you, it is essential to work with an experienced, compassionate, creative, and flexible celebrant. Because you are dealing with some of the most profound issues of your life, choose a guide you trust and who is on your side. There can be considerable pressure on both bride and groom on your wedding day, so be sure to select someone with whom you're comfortable. You need a celebrant who is willing to devote sufficient time to help you develop the ceremony you want. For ideas on how to find a celebrant, see chapter 17.
- A celebrant who is willing to accept *your* needs and help you develop your ideas is not always easy to find, so we recommend that you start looking early. If you are marrying someone of another faith, the clergy you were counting on may not be willing to perform the ceremony. Be sure you are clear about what you want and what the celebrant is and is not willing to do.

3. Who will conduct your wedding ceremony—the celebrant or you?

- Do you want the celebrant to read the entire ceremony so that all you have to do is say "I do"?
- Do you want to express your own feelings, philosophies, and vows, and have the celebrant there only as the witness for the state?

- Do you want to share responsibility for conducting the ceremony with the celebrant?
- Because many couples feel shy about speaking in front of a group, they choose to have the celebrant do most of the talking. Often, they make this choice too quickly and then regret that they did not attempt a more active role. Don't deprive yourselves of a moving and meaningful ceremony in which you, the couple, give full expression to your deepest thoughts and feelings. We'll show you many ways to ease the anxiety, and we'll even offer some remedies for stage fright (see chapter 16).

4. *How large a wedding party do you want and who will be in it?*

- Will you have just one witness, or a best man and maid/matron of honor, or a larger party including parents, bridesmaids and groomsmen, and flower and ring bearers?
- Who will sign as legal witnesses—your best man and maid/matron of honor, or will you choose a parent, sibling, or someone else?
- Will there be children in the wedding party? Children certainly add charm and warmth to a ceremony, but they may also add an element of surprise. If the children are very young, shy, or impulsive, be prepared for the unexpected and accept it with good humor. Some children may not want to participate. Don't pressure them. If you do include young children, we recommend having someone in charge of them.
- Will your budget accommodate all the people you want to have stand up with you? Although it's nice to have many friends in the wedding party, it will add to your expense and increase the work.
- Is the size of the wedding party appropriate to the site? A large party in a small space may crowd you—the bride and groom—from being the center of attention.

- Is the size of the wedding party suitable for the degree of formality you have chosen? A large group of attendants for a small, intimate ceremony may be unwieldy and out of character.

5. *What role will friends and relatives have in your ceremony?*

- Are there friends or family members who won't be in the wedding party, but whom you'd like to include in the ceremony?
- What role do you want your parents to play?
- Do either of you have children you want to include in the ceremony? Do they want to be included? There are many roles for them in addition to flower girl or boy, or ring bearer.
- Will your guests be active participants or observers? Do you have friends or relatives who could participate as musicians, poets or readers, photographers, or sound techs? Responsive readings, spontaneous wishes, and shared wine or flower rituals are just a few of the ways your guests can contribute to your ceremony.
- Will you need to give tasks or special care to any potentially troublesome people in order to channel their energies in constructive ways?
- Innumerable tasks will be available for willing hands. Be prepared to ask for help and delegate responsibility. Most people appreciate being asked.

6. *What music, if any, will you include in the ceremony?*

Music has great power to influence human emotions and will help develop the mood you want, adding to the tone and drama of your wedding. We'll provide some specific suggestions later in the book. Do you prefer pop, rock, jazz, classical, or traditional wedding selections?

- Will you choose something that has special significance for the two of you?

- Will it be live or taped, vocal or instrumental? If live, how will you find the performers? How much are you willing to spend? If recorded, who will be in charge of starting and stopping the tape or CD at the right time?
- Do you want music before, during, and after the ceremony? What selections will you choose to begin and end the ceremony itself? Is there a favorite piece you want to include?
- Live performers, especially if they are talented friends, provide unusual pleasure. It's helpful if the musicians are available for the rehearsal.
- One caution: When the wedding party has to stand through a long instrumental selection, it can feel quite awkward and uncomfortable to everyone—observers as well as participants.

7. *Who's invited?*

There are benefits to a small ceremony: a sense of intimacy and involvement with the people who are closest to you. There are also virtues in inviting a large number of guests: more of your community gets to participate, nobody's feelings get hurt, it may add drama to the occasion. The size of your guest list may require difficult choices. Your earlier decisions regarding the purpose and mood of your ceremony—and your budget—may guide you.

- Will you have only family and intimate friends, or will you invite all your acquaintances and business associates?
- How will you decide where to draw the line? If you do not invite some people, will their feelings be hurt? How will you deal with this?
- Will some be invited only to the reception or only to the ceremony?
- Sometimes economics require a smaller invitation list than you would like. It's more important to include the people you really care about than to stage a big party. Consider creative options to save money. Use balloons

instead of flowers, recorded instead of live music, a potluck instead of a caterer, your backyard instead of a rented facility, or ask friends to photograph and videotape your ceremony.

8. *What kind of wedding invitations and announcements do you want?*

Keep in mind the general mood you want for the wedding. How can the design of your invitation help to establish this mood right from the start?

- Will you design your own, have an artistic friend design one for you, or use commercially available invitations? Will they be formal or informal? Printed, engraved, handwritten, computer generated, photocopied? Or will you invite people by telephone or e-mail?
- Will you send wedding announcements to those not invited to the ceremony or reception?

ॐ ॐ ॐ

Take a moment to look back over your notes, and highlight the ideas you like best. Then put your notebook away for a few days. Taking a fresh look later will give you the opportunity to fine-tune and reevaluate your choices.

Use your preferences to guide your initial decisions. You'll be referring to them again in other chapters as you start to write your ceremony.

*When the one man loves the one woman
and the one woman loves the one man,
the very angels desert heaven
and sit in that house and sing for joy.*
—Brahma Sutra

Chapter 3

Choosing the Members
of the Wedding

Your wealth is where your friends are.
—Plautus

Think carefully about choosing the members of your wedding party. Be creative in the way you select roles for each person. Honor friends and family by asking them to participate. There are more details than you can handle yourselves; therefore, delegate responsibility freely.

ॐ ॐ ॐ

The Wedding Couple

This is your day! You should be able to relax and enjoy it. Don't load yourselves down with last-minute details. The bride and groom sometimes feel so rushed and hassled they get distracted from the meaning of their ceremony. Plan carefully and you can avoid the overload. You can use a professional wedding coordinator, or assign details to your relatives and your best friends and give them the authority to make decisions for you.

For example, make preliminary arrangements for the favors and centerpieces and then ask your sister or your maid of honor to see that they are placed neatly on each table. Order your flowers well in advance. If the florist doesn't deliver, ask an usher or a bridesmaid to pick them up. Your task is to look at the big picture and plan the whole event. Arrange for others to assist you and to handle the details. And when you have delegated responsibility to someone, trust them to accomplish it!

Decide whether you want to see each other before the ceremony. For some, not seeing each other beforehand heightens the anticipation and adds significance to their coming together at the ceremony. Others may gain calm and comfort from being together before this most significant event. Either way, take time to relax, meditate, or do whatever makes you feel good. Quiet time beforehand will reduce your stress and remind you of the importance of what you are about to do—the reasons you are getting married, and the deep connection between you. You'll experience the deeper meaning of this event and not be distracted by petty details. This is your wedding; make it the one you want.

ॐ ॐ ॐ

Attendants of Honor

You will probably choose best friends or close family members as your attendants of honor—but you don't have to limit yourselves to the traditional gender roles. It's up to you if you want your best man to be a woman, or your maid of honor to be your man of honor. These two attendants will be your primary supporters before, during, and after the ceremony. They can take on many of the details of the wedding preparations.

Your chief attendants will be with you during the sometimes strained time before the ceremony; they'll take charge of the wedding rings and stand with you during the ceremony. The attendant of honor holds the bride's bouquet during the ring exchange and other rituals, and makes sure that the bride's wedding gown train is neatly arranged. The best man/woman usually gives the celebrant the fee and traditionally gives the first toast during the reception. Most often, these two sign the marriage license as witnesses—although sometimes the wedding couple will choose to select some other friend or relative for this honor.

ॐ ॐ ॐ

Other Attendants

Friends or relatives who serve as your attendants enjoy a distinct honor. In selecting them you are telling them that you care about them, trust them, and need them by your side during these special moments.

In traditional ceremonies, the ushers escort guests to their seats. The bridesmaids act as ladies-in-waiting to the bride—helping her to dress, fixing her hair, doing last-minute chores, and so on.

In contemporary weddings the attendants frequently take an active part in the ceremony. They might read poetry, sing, or offer good wishes. You may want to ask your attendants for their help in the wedding preparations—perhaps to take charge of some aspect of the decorations, food, or music.

Although traditionally the bride has only female attendants and the groom has male attendants, you are free to choose your attendants based on your feelings toward them.

ॐ ॐ ॐ

Parents of the Couple

Creating a significant role for your parents in your ceremony is one of the most pleasing gifts you can give them. In certain ethnic traditions—for example, in Chinese and Jewish weddings—both sets of parents accompany their children during the processional. In contemporary weddings, parents may stand with the wedding party, welcome their new son or daughter into their family, read poetry, or offer good wishes.

We think that you should seriously question the ritual of "giving away" the bride. Customs and roles have changed over time, and you should consider whether this practice is appropriate for you. Many modern couples are dismayed at the implication that the bride is "property" to be handed over to the groom by the father. Others take comfort in having the bride's father perform this traditional role. With a little ingenuity you can create alternative ways to acknowledge and honor your father—and your mother.

Although your parents will be honored guests at your wedding, they may also assist you with the preparations. They will feel needed if you ask them to perform necessary tasks. Define the task and the way you want it done, then let your folks take over. Parents are often adept at overseeing last-minute details. Things may not get done *exactly* the way you want, but your parents will probably do their tasks well and will feel good about being active participants in your wedding. Their collaboration may avoid many of the hassles that occur when people are under stress and coping with differences in values, expectations, and approaches.

It is especially important to determine the differences between what your parents expect and what *you* want from *your* wedding. You may confront special situations such as accommodating divorced parents, multiple stepparents, or parents with differing religious or social values.

Before anyone gets hot under the collar, determine whether you can reconcile your parents' wishes with your own. If so, there is no problem. Unfortunately, you and your parents may hold so tightly to your own convictions that your worlds seem threatened by any compromise. Step back and assess whether the issue is indeed fundamental. If it's not, try to negotiate or trade off.

Conflict may arise over something as simple as whether the clothing should be formal or casual. Search for some middle ground. Clothing could be less formal than your mother wants, but not as casual as you'd prefer. Serious controversy may erupt over more significant issues, such as conflicting traditions in interfaith marriages, but these too can often be resolved. In one situation, the bride's Jewish mother strongly resented the inclusion of a New Testament reading requested by the groom's Catholic family. She finally relented when they agreed to also include the breaking of the wine glass, a traditional Jewish custom.

An even more difficult issue to resolve is when a parent insists on a religious ceremony, but the couple favors a secular service. In every situation where conflict arises, try to find a compromise that everyone can live with. If everyone can agree that your larger purpose is the same, and that the only disagreement is about *form,* perhaps all parties will be less likely to feel personally threatened. Take a deep breath and explore ways in which both your position and theirs can be honored.

Don't push on the wall when there might be a door. If the circle of their arguments shuts you out, try to draw a bigger circle that includes everyone. Seek a solution in which everyone wins. You can afford to give up *some* of your notions; but remember, it's your wedding and you cannot compromise your basic ideals.

ॐ ॐ ॐ

Junior Bridesmaids and Ushers, Flower Girl/Boy and Ring Bearer

These roles offer a wonderful opportunity to include young children in the wedding party. They are especially meaningful if either wedding partner has children. There are other ways children can help make the wedding a more festive occasion. For instance, have the children greet guests as they arrive, and have them hand out such things as flowers, groom's cake, a program or copy of the ceremony, or birdseed to throw at the couple after the reception.

Remember that young children are unpredictable. Under tension, they may refuse to perform. Four-year-olds may burst into tears and run to Grandma just when you want them to walk sedately down the aisle. Children may fidget or walk away instead of standing still. Children can add much delight to your ceremony if you allow for the unexpected.

ॐ ॐ ॐ

Guests

If your guests are passive witnesses to your ceremony, their only task is to be attentive to the words spoken. If they are active participants, you can offer them an opportunity to share thoughts and good wishes during the ceremony; take part in a wine or candle ritual; form a circle around the bride and groom; pass a kiss; or cooperate in a responsive reading. The possibilities are limited only by your ingenuity.

ॐ ॐ ॐ

Celebrant

Your wedding will not be legal without the presence of an authorized celebrant, except in rare circumstances.

The celebrant is especially important in a ceremony that you are writing yourselves. You will turn to this person for help, ideas, inspiration and support, so establish a good rapport. In the best contemporary weddings, the celebrant will encourage you to write much of the ceremony; most celebrants will urge that, at the least, you write your own vows. Although the celebrant might be willing to write the entire ceremony for you, we strongly recommend that you both be actively involved in the creative process. Otherwise, you may end up with the celebrant's wedding ceremony and not your own.

It is not always easy to find a celebrant who is willing to participate in creative and innovative wedding ceremonies (see chapter 17). Start your search early. Offer a fee that is commensurate with the importance of the celebrant to this rite of passage. In a small ceremony, the celebrant may not need to spend much time or energy and may be willing to perform the ceremony for a minimal fee. If you are having an elaborate ceremony, expect to pay a more substantial fee. Even if the celebrant has a standard fee, it is common courtesy to add a bonus for special services rendered. You should also expect to pay for any special costs incurred by the celebrant, such as travel or overnight accommodations.

ॐ ॐ ॐ

Musicians, Poets, and Readers

These are the cameo roles in your ceremony that add depth and significance. Audition the musicians before you hire them. Don't hire your cousin's best friend's nephew sight unseen (or unheard). Make certain that the musicians are familiar with your selections, and understand when, where, how, and for how long you want them to play.

If you are including poetry or other readings, make sure that both you and the reader are comfortable with the selections chosen and with the ability of the reader.

ॐॐॐॐॐ

There is nothing on this earth more
to be prized than true friendship.
—St. Thomas Aquinas

Chapter 4

Designing and Writing Your Ceremony

...Biting my truant pen, beating myself for spite:
Fool! said my Muse to me,
look in thy heart and write.

—Sir Philip Sidney

Anne Lamott tells a wonderful story about facing a large and overwhelming writing project. Her brother, then ten, had to write a report about birds. He procrastinated until the last night, feeling helpless about how to accomplish this huge task. Finally, his father sat down beside him, put his arm around his shoulders and said, "Bird by bird, buddy. Just take it bird by bird."

We're going to help you design and write your ceremony "bird by bird"—one section at a time. We recommend that you start well in advance of the wedding date, because the more time you allow, the finer your fine-tuning will be. But even if time is short, we'll show you how you can accomplish the task.

The most important thing to remember when you begin to write is to say what's important to you. If there is a primary rule, it is *be authentic*. Your guests are present to celebrate your happiness with you and they wish you the best. They are not critics; they are not a jury. The most moving and memorable weddings occur when the couple speaks simply, directly, and from the heart. There's no need to be a poet or novelist, and no need to use lofty language; just be yourselves. Your wedding ceremony can feel original, fresh, and comfortable, yet still be serious.

Before you write your final version, you will probably have a lot of mental clutter to get out of the way. Although it may sound odd, we recommend that you write down the clutter—to get it out and get past it. Don't criticize yourselves; don't try to find the perfect words the first time. Just write. No one else will see your rough draft. When you read it over a day or so later, keep the pieces you like and toss the rest. Write some more and then repeat the same steps. The more you allow yourselves to write it all down, let it simmer, then reread and edit—then write some more—the more likely you'll get it just the way you want it.

Start by writing short, declarative sentences—simple and direct. You may start with just a word or a fragment of a sentence. That's fine. Write it down in any form you can for the first draft. Don't try to organize. Simply put your next thought down on the paper. You may find a selection in this book that exactly expresses what you want. Use it. Some of our selections may inspire you to write your own thoughts in your own words.

The more choices you make as you go along, and the more ideas you put into words, the better. At each step of this process we suggest that you talk, write, and then set aside your writing for a couple of days. When your mind is fresh again, review what you've written and add, delete, change, and fine tune. When it seems to say what you want it to say, ask your celebrant to read it, edit it, and make suggestions. You may also want to ask a trusted and especially literate friend to review your draft and give you feedback.

Keep your notebook handy, because you are going to use all the information you've gathered, the decisions you've made, and the dreams you've described. As you go along, be sure to write down particular thoughts, phrases, or words that you find meaningful.

ॐ ॐ ॐ

Choosing Your Ceremony's Components

Every wedding ceremony has a structure. Some parts—the opening, the exchange of vows, and the closing—are essential and have a logical order in the ceremony. Other elements, such as the celebrant's address, the ring exchange, and other significant rituals, often are dictated by tradition or taste. Some components are more a matter of style and preference. You can include them or not, and they can be placed within the ceremony wherever appropriate. These would include statements of appreciation, poetry, music, and family participation.

Each of these units can be written separately, then shuffled, combined, and recombined until you are satisfied with the arrangement. Think of a wedding ceremony as consisting of the following components:

1. The essential structure of the ceremony

- The opening
- The vows
- The closing

2. Significant elements that are usually included

- The celebrant's address
- Couple's statements of appreciation
- Ring or wine rituals

3. Other segments that add richness and meaning

- Additional rituals
- Family participation
- Poetry, prose, and music

Your own preferences will determine which of these parts you use, and their order of appearance.

The following chapters will take these components one at a time. We'll help you decide what you want to convey, give suggestions for how to tackle the task of writing, and provide examples to help get your creative juices flowing.

We'll start with the two most personal and important components, your expressions of appreciation and your vows.

ᘏᘏᘏᘏᘏ

Then, rising with Aurora's light,
The Muse invok'd, sit down to write;
Blot out, correct, insert, refine,
Enlarge, diminish, interline.
                              —Jonathan Swift

Chapter 5

Writing Your Statements
of Appreciation

I am not sure that Earth is round
Nor that the sky is really blue.
The tale of why the apples fall
May or may not be true.
I do not know what makes the tides
Nor what tomorrow's world may do,
But I have certainty enough,
For I am sure of you.
—Amelia Josephine Burr

By starting to write your ceremony with the appreciations, you will focus your attention on the most important element of your relationship—your love for each other. Expressing what you love about each other early in the preparation of the ceremony lays the groundwork for the promises you will make, and allows your writing to flow more easily.

Your statements of appreciation are a deeply moving part of the contemporary wedding ceremony. These statements may express how you met; what you love about each other; your philosophies of life, love, and marriage; or your hopes and expectations of each other and your marriage. They may be your personal expressions, or the words of a famous poet or author.

What do you want to say in your statements to each other? We'll provide a series of questions for you to think about, discuss, and then decide. Even if you don't intend to include statements of appreciation in your ceremony, we urge you to spend time considering these issues anyway. The questions will help you think about the amazing and wonderful person you are about to marry, encourage you to learn more about each other, and help you identify the reasons you love each other so much. Some of the questions go right to the heart of what brought you together and what holds you together. Some ask you to think about and discuss aspects of your relationship that often don't get discussed until *after* the wedding. By then, the things you love about each other can also become the things that drive you nuts. Exploring these qualities before you get married will lay a foundation for talking about them later in a productive way.

As you talk, jot down memories that delight you, events that confirm your love for each other, creative ways in which you've solved problems together, qualities that make your partner the person of your dreams. Note any words, phrases, or sentences that express the special feeling you have for your partner. Use these notes to help you write both your statements and your vows.

ॐ ॐ ॐ

Exploring Your Relationship

1. *How did the two of you meet and what first attracted you to each other?*

   What are your most vivid memories of that first meeting? What was your first reaction to your partner?

2. *What is your fondest memory of your courtship?*

   When did you know you were meant to be together? What made you feel you were on cloud nine?

3. **What do you love most about your partner?**

Be specific. Think of his or her character, thoughtful gestures, and the way you feel special when you are together.

4. **What is your partner's greatest strength?**

What are the qualities that you cherish, admire, and respect that he or she brings to your relationship? What qualities will contribute to your happiness and enhance the commitment and abiding love between you?

5. **What obstacles did the two of you overcome in your courtship?**

How did these experiences strengthen the bond between you? What did you learn about the strengths and weaknesses each of you brings to the relationship?

6. **What has your partner contributed to your life so far?**

In what ways has your partner added to your health, happiness, and success? How will being married make each of you a better person?

7. **What words best describe your partner?**

Think about your partner's strengths, weaknesses, likes, and dislikes. Be concrete and detailed. What things make your relationship hum and what things cause discord? How does your partner contribute to your personal world and to the world at large?

8. **What do the two of you love to do together?**

What hobbies, activities, interests, customs, and dreams do you share? Do you like the same books, sports, movies? Do you love to dine out or travel together? Are you both exhilarated by nature, the outdoors, hiking, biking, skiing, camping? How about spending time with friends or family, window-shopping, cooking, reading together, cuddling? What common goals are you working toward? Are you planning a family, saving for the future, advancing social reform, or pursuing spiritual growth? Think about the things that enrich your lives together.

9. *Do the two of you share the same religious, spiritual, or philosophical beliefs?*

Be specific about what you share—and what you don't. Do you both feel as strongly about your commitments? How will you accommodate and respect your areas of difference? What will you agree to disagree about? Which disagreements may result in an ongoing struggle?

10. *Do you both want children?*

Do you agree on when and how many? Are you in accord about how you will raise them, and what kind of discipline you believe in? What about their religious training?

ॐ ॐ ॐ

Writing Your Appreciations

After you have discussed and taken notes on the most important facets of your love for each other, you are ready to start writing. Use your own words or find inspiration from poets or authors.

Start by focusing on the mood you want to create with your ceremony: intimate, philosophical, reverential, joyous...? In an intimate ceremony, you might want to speak personally to each other about your love and your dreams. In a philosophical wedding, you might focus on what marriage means to each of you. The kind of language you choose is significant. Intimate language will be personal and express warmth and tenderness; philosophical language may be more idealistic and lofty.

Remember that as you speak to each other, you will also be speaking to your guests. To make your ceremony personal, authentic, and touching, take the risk of going public with what has been private. Use simple language that feels comfortable, natural, and honest to you.

ॐ ॐ ॐ

Examples of Appreciations

TO EACH OTHER

Brief and personal

GROOM

> Jerri, you are loving, caring, and strong. I trust you and know that together, we can live life fully. I cannot imagine a future without you. I look forward to growing old with you, and falling in love over and over again.

BRIDE

> Roy, standing here with you creates an immeasurable feeling of peace and tranquility in my heart and in my soul. You are my companion, my confidant, my playmate, and my lover. You are my best friend, and today you become my husband.
>
> In marrying you, I look forward to sharing our dreams and our lives.

ॐॐॐॐॐ

How do I love thee?

GROOM

> Janet, I love you for many reasons, especially because you accept me the way I am. You show respect for my family, my friends, and for me, and you share my dreams.
>
> I love your independence and that you are resourceful, considerate, and beautiful. I love you and want to marry you.

BRIDE

> Quang, you are smart, tender and lots of fun. You are a good cook and a great dancer. You believe in the importance of family, and I know you will create a loving home for our children. We share the same hopes and dreams. I love you most of all because you are my best friend.

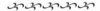

Mutual Admiration

GROOM

Carrie, you are my best friend, the sun that shines in my life, the other half that makes me whole, your smile lights up my day.

You give me comfort, unconditional love, and the security to be myself. You make me laugh and feel alive. I'm happy to begin and end each day with you. With you, I am complete.

BRIDE

Joshua, you mean the world to me. I am going to tell you what I love most about you.

I love your sense of humor. You are constantly putting a smile on my face and providing me with my daily dose of laughter.

I love your daily compliments; you make me feel so special.

I love your smile; you brighten my day. When I am not with you, just the thought of you makes me feel good about everything. I admire your ambition and your desire to succeed and, at the same time, your ability to have fun and enjoy life.

I truly believe that I am the luckiest girl to have found you. I am so excited and happy to spend the rest of my life with you. I love you with all of my heart and soul.

The second time around

GROOM

Pat, I never expected to find love again. However, sitting next to me on an airplane, you revived my hope and excitement. You are a wonderful woman who knows how to accept love and to give love in return. I want to spend the rest of my life with you.

I hope that our families and friends will share in our happiness with us. Thank you so much for accepting my love and joining me in marriage today. I love you very much.

BRIDE

Lewis, in just eight months we have discovered a wonderful relationship that weaves a rich tapestry of similar lifetime choices and experiences. You possess the key that unlocked my heart and soul.

I love you for your sensitivity to my highs and lows; your concern for all facets of our daily life; and our enjoyment of music and dancing and observing nature in the garden and from the tops of mountains.

I love your mischievous spirit and dry sense of humor. I love your thoughtful concerns for our extended family. I love sharing our creative energies for cooking and photography.

Together we have a rhythm that makes us one.

ॐॐॐॐॐ

Appreciations for an older couple

GROOM *(Sonnet 30, William Shakespeare)*
> *When to the sessions of sweet silent thought*
> *I summon up remembrance of things past,*
> *I sigh the lack of many a thing I sought,*
> *And with old woes new wail my dear time's waste:*
> *Then can I drown an eye, unused to flow,*
> *For precious friends hid in death's dateless night,*
> *And weep afresh love's long since cancelled woe,*
> *And moan the expense of many a vanished sight:*
> *Then can I grieve at grievances foregone,*
> *And heavily from woe to woe tell o'er*
> *The sad account of fore-bemoanèd moan,*
> *Which I new pay as if not paid before.*
> > *But if the while I think on thee, dear friend,*
> > *All losses are restor'd and sorrows end.*

BRIDE *(Sonnet 19, William Shakespeare)*
> *Devouring Time, blunt thou the lion's paws,*
> *And make the earth devour her own sweet brood;*
> *Pluck the keen teeth from the fierce tiger's jaws,*
> *And burn the long-lived phoenix in her blood;*

Make glad and sorry seasons as thou fleet'st,
And do whate'er thou wilt, swift-footed Time,
To the wide world and all her fading sweets.
But I forbid thee one most heinous crime:
O, carve not with thy hours my love's fair brow,
Nor draw no lines there with thine antique pen;
Him in thy course untainted do allow
For beauty's pattern to succeeding men.
    Yet do the worst, Old Time; despite thy wrong,
    My love shall in my verse ever live young.

ﾊﾟﾊﾟﾊﾟﾊﾟﾊﾟ

PARTNER 1 (*Making Contact,* Virginia Satir)
I want to love you without clutching, appreciate you without judging, join you without invading, invite you without demanding, criticize you without blaming, and help you without insulting. If I can have the same from you then we can truly meet and enrich each other.

PARTNER 2 (from *Oath of Friendship,* Arthur Waley, translator)
I want to be your friend
For ever and ever without break or decay.
When the hills are all flat
And the rivers are all dry,
When it lightens and thunders in winter,
When it rains and snows in summer,
When Heaven and Earth mingle—
Not till then will I part from you.

ﾊﾟﾊﾟﾊﾟﾊﾟﾊﾟ

A Poem Read Alternately by the Couple (*Love,* Roy Croft)

BRIDE
I love you,
Not only for what you are,
But for what I am
When I am with you.

GROOM

I love you,
Not only for what
You have made of yourself
But for what
You are making of me.

BRIDE

I love you
For the part of me
That you bring out.
I love you
For putting your hand
Into my heaped up heart
And passing over
All the foolish weak things
That you can't help
Seeing, dimly there,
And for drawing out
Into the light
All the beautiful belongings
That no one else has looked
Quite far enough to find.

GROOM

I love you because you
Are helping me to make
Of the lumber of my life,
Not a tavern,
But a temple;
Out of the works
Of my every day,
Not a reproach
But a song.

BRIDE

I love you
Because you have done
More than any creed

Could have done
To make me happy.
You have done it without a touch,
Without a word
Without a sign.
You have done it
By being yourself.

BOTH
Perhaps that is what being a friend means after all.

Cherishing each other

GROOM

Erika, you are everything I could ask for in a wife. You are thoughtful, loving, honest, and above all, you are my friend.

I accept you now for who you are and for who you will become. With you, I look forward to the future, to sharing our sorrows and celebrating our triumphs, to learning more about each other, and to growing old together. I want nothing more than to share my life with you, in your loving arms.

BRIDE

Greg, you have become my closest friend. I look forward to waking up by your side each morning, and to returning to the warmth of your arms at the end of each day.

I love your humor, your cheerfulness, your intelligence, your creativity, your silliness, and your peaceful nature. I feel honored to take you as my husband, and I know that our children will be blessed with a wonderful father. Together, we have more strength and creativity than we ever had on our own.

In which each party repeats the same words

The couple repeats the following to each other.

I am proud to become your spouse. Where there have been tears, I will offer you laughter; where there has been pain, I will offer you kindness and love. Where there are memories, I will open to you, and I will share freely with you our real treasure: the tomorrows we will have as husband and wife. Today and always, I offer you my love.

TO THE GUESTS

In which the couple tell their guests why they are marrying

GROOM

We have asked you to come together to witness our marriage and celebrate with us our joy and happiness. Teri and I have found in each other a spirit of joy, a sense of shared purposes and world views, a companionship, a love so strong and so vital that we wish to join our lives.

BRIDE

We enter upon our marriage eagerly and with a profound sense of joy. Our worlds will continue to enlarge; our interests and our circle of friends have already been enhanced and expanded. Your delight and approval—so warmly expressed—has greatly enriched our happiness.

Love: A responsive reading involving the couple and the guests

This responsive reading was printed in the wedding program that was distributed prior to the ceremony.

GROOM

Barbara and I have found love with each other, and today we will become husband and wife. We know that our love for each other is an extension of the love we have been given by all of you, our families and friends. After we are married we will continue to seek the love and support of each of you because we know we cannot survive in isolation. Please join us now as we speak of the art of love.

BRIDE

Tom and I know that happiness in marriage is not something that just happens. We know we must create our marriage and learn ways to show each other love, so that our relationship will never grow stale.

GUESTS

Love is giving and generous and kind.

GROOM

Love is saying "I love you" each day.

GUESTS

Love is for always and forever. It is remembering, even during the hard times or the angry times, that this is your beloved and your friend.

BRIDE

Love is appreciation of the big and little things that your partner does each day, and the generous demonstration of that appreciation through words and acts.

GUESTS

Love is accepting each other's imperfections. It is developing patience, flexibility, and a sense of humor, so you can laugh together at life's absurdities.

GROOM

Love is not taking the other for granted. It is taking the time to keep the courtship alive, in spite of other responsibilities and demands.

GUESTS

Love is finding delight in common interests and pursuits. It is sharing values and goals.

BRIDE

Love is giving to each other and doing things for each other, not out of duty but with a sense of joy.

GUESTS

Love is creating a relationship in which the independence is equal, the dependence is mutual, and the obligation is reciprocal.

GROOM

Love is not only marrying the right partner, it is being the right partner.

GUESTS

Love is fostered in a circle of love that gathers in family and friends. Your marriage will flourish in the midst of a loving community. We are your friends, we pledge you our love and support.

ぷぷぷぷぷ

That is the true season of love,
when we believe that we alone can love,
that no one could ever have loved so before us,
and no one will love in the same way after us.
—Johann Wolfgang von Goethe

Chapter 6

Writing Your Vows

When you love someone, you love
the whole person, just as he or she is,
and not as you would like them to be.
—Leo Tolstoy

A vow is a solemn promise to dedicate yourself to an act, a service, or a way of life. For most people, the marriage vows are a promise of love and fidelity. For many, the vows are a promise to God. In your vows you will give voice to your commitments to each other. In addition, the vows are your legal agreement to take each other as husband and wife.

Traditionally, the words of these vows have been prescribed, and they have been nearly identical for both bride and groom. Today, the vows are frequently different, symbolizing the individuality of each person and the acceptance of these differences within the relationship. Vows may reflect your personal wishes, expectations, and promises, or they may be symbolic and generalized.

We believe that the wedding vows are the essence of your ceremony and form a fundamental building block for your marriage. Take them seriously and they will form the foundation of a lasting and successful marriage. The vows are so important that we recommend that you take special care in planning how you will express them. Ideally, you will know them so well that you will be able to look at each other, perhaps hold hands, and pay attention to the promises you make. A cue card will assure you that you won't forget the words.

ॐ ॐ ॐ

Exploring the Basis for Your Vows

The questions below will help you focus on the meaning of your vows.

1. *What marriage vows are you willing to make? Is marriage "till death do us part," or merely "as long as love shall last"?*

   There's a lot of evidence that couples who vow to make their relationship work, no matter what, and who believe that marriage vows are "for better and for worse" have a stronger chance of their marriage surviving hard times. Do you both see your vows in the same way? What reservations, if any, do you have? How will you work through hard times, disagreements, hurts, betrayals, or losses?

2. *What expectations do each of you have of marriage? In what ways will marriage change your relationship and your lives?*

   Think about your differences and similarities. Explore the responsibilities each of you will take in the nitty-gritty business of living together, making decisions, raising children, getting the chores done, and spending and saving money.

   One of the best of ways to discover potential strengths and difficulties is to remember how your parents related to each other, because they are your basic role models. How will you be like or unlike them? What is there about the relationship between your partner's parents that you especially like or dislike? If either or both of you have been married before, think about what worked and what didn't work in that relationship, and how you want this relationship to be different.

As you talk together, pay attention to how the two of you deal with differences. Are you able to listen to each other, even when you don't agree? Is there understanding, respect, and tolerance for your differences? Are you able to negotiate and find solutions that allow both of you to feel good about the outcome? If not, are you able to accept your partner's position and live with it even if you don't agree? The ability to resolve problems respectfully is a crucial ingredient in a healthy and durable relationship.

3. *What are the key components that will make your marriage endure?*

If your commitment is to make this marriage last a lifetime, what is the source of the strength that will enable you both to work through life's problems and heartaches? What will the two of you bring to each other to help strengthen your marriage, your commitment, and your love? Is there something special about the way you show each other love, respect, and admiration? Do you have a belief system that will further your strength and resolve? Have you worked out a successful strategy for resolving differences and solving problems together? Are there dreams or goals that bind you together? If you have difficulties resolving differences or being respectful even when you are angry with each other, will you each agree to get outside help before serious problems arise? Whom will you choose for such help—your clergy, a marriage counselor, a good friend, a close relative?

4. *Do you want to make nearly identical vows, or do you want them to reflect your individuality?*

Historically, vows have been similar, though with some significant differences. The man promised to "love, honor and cherish" while the woman promised to "love, honor, and obey." Because the idea of the woman obeying the man isn't a widely held value today, you won't hear "obey" very often in modern ceremonies. Although vows that are nearly the same are still the mainstay of traditional ceremonies, in contemporary weddings there is a preference for each to make promises in their own words.

≈ ≈ ≈

Wording Your Promises

Give yourself time to think through what you want to promise. Then write whatever comes to mind without worrying about whether it's good or bad. Speak from your heart. Write simple, declarative sentences that express what you are truly willing to promise your partner. When you have written as much as you can, leave the first draft behind for a while, and return to it a day or two later. When you are ready to proceed, review and change your first draft, adding whatever comes to mind. Again put it aside for a day or so. Repeat this process until you have your best ideas on paper. Let them sit for a few more days, until you're ready to start editing and polishing your vows.

≈ ≈ ≈

Examples of Vows

TRADITIONAL VOWS

CELEBRANT *(to the groom)*
Wilt thou have this woman to thy wedded wife, to live together after God's ordinance in the holy estate of matrimony? Wilt thou love her, comfort her, honor, and keep her in sickness and in health: and, forsaking all other, keep thee only unto her, so long as ye both shall live?

GROOM
I will.

CELEBRANT *(to the bride)*

Wilt thou have this man to thy wedded husband, to live together after God's ordinance in the holy estate of matrimony? Wilt thou obey him, and serve him, love, honor, and keep him in sickness and in health: and, forsaking all other, keep thee only unto him, so long as ye both shall live?

BRIDE

I will.

సఁసఁసఁసఁసఁ

GROOM

I, David, take thee, Julia, to be my wedded wife; to have and to hold, from this day forward; for better, for worse; for richer, for poorer; in sickness and in health; to love and to cherish 'til death do us part.

BRIDE

I, Julia, take thee, David, to be my wedded husband; to have and to hold, from this day forward; for better, for worse; for richer, for poorer; in sickness and in health; to love and to cherish 'til death do us part.

ॐ ॐ ॐ

EXPRESSING DIFFERENT PROMISES

CELEBRANT

Martin and Maia, of the billions of people who inhabit our planet, you have found and chosen each other! It is appropriate that your unique relationship brings you to the milestone we celebrate today. You have been through many changes together during the past three years, and you remain remarkably compatible and comfortable with each other, sharing good cheer, significant values, and an enduring desire to establish your own family. Your relationship abounds with good will. Although you differ one from the other, you have found much of value in common: your humor, your ability to communicate, your shared wish to live each moment fully. Turn to each other now and make the promises that will commit you to each other from this day forth.

GROOM

Maia, I promise always to love, honor, and protect you; to promote your dreams and aspirations; to share in your triumphs and failures; to be true to myself and true to you; to cherish your laughter and your beautiful smile; to build a loving family; and to nurture our love forever. I say these things with all my heart.

BRIDE

Martin, in marrying you, I commit to loving you unconditionally, through the ordinary, the extraordinary and the trying moments of our lives; to communicate with you openly and honestly; to encourage our growth—not only as a couple, but as individuals; to create a strong and loving family together; and to be your best friend, your lover, and your wife.

ぁぁぁぁぁ

GROOM

Zoë, I promise to strengthen our love with every passing day, to listen to you with my heart, to catch you if you fall, to fill your life with love and never stop loving you.

BRIDE

Michael, I promise you that I will always hold your dreams in my heart, be a source of strength and tenderness for you, respect the sanctity of our relationship, and build a legacy of love that we will pass on to our family.

ぁぁぁぁぁ

PARTNER 1

Jaynee, I love, respect, and honor you above all others, and I am committed to our partnership in life. I promise to express my thoughts and emotions to you, and to listen to you in times of joy and in times of sorrow. I will strive to broaden our horizons, expand our boundaries, and explore the wonders of life with you. From this day forward, I will join you as your life companion, offering to you the essence of all that I am.

PARTNER 2

Michelle, I have chosen you—my best friend, my love—to be my life's partner. I want to grow beside you and to be with you in all our changing selves. I promise to cherish and respect you, to be steadfast and loyal to you, and to be sensitive to your needs. I promise you my love and understanding, through both sorrow and celebration. From this day forward, I will be your companion, and strive to fill our lives together with happiness, adventure, and peace. Now there will be no more you; and no more me; but only us.

ॐॐॐॐॐ

BRIDE

I, Betty Smith, do take thee, Barton Jones, to be my lawfully wedded husband. To share the joys and sorrows of our unfolding tomorrows and in all ways that I know or may be shown, to give of myself for you and our family.

GROOM

I, Barton Jones, do take thee, Betty Smith, to be the wife of my days, to be the mother of my children, to be the companion of my house. We shall share what trouble and sorrow may come our way, and we shall share our store of goodness and plenty and love.

ॐॐॐॐॐ

BRIDE

Alan, I commit my life and love to you, and to this union between us.

I will respect your individuality, and accept your feelings, although, at times, they may differ from mine. I will respond to our differences as a way to broaden our views, not narrow them.

I will lovingly and joyously share in your successes. I will strive to fulfill your needs. I promise patience and flexibility in resolving our conflicts.

I shall never abuse your love, or take it for granted, for I know that the love I receive is equal to the love I give.

It is to you that I pledge my love.

GROOM

Kelli, it is with excitement and joy that I embark on this new direction in my life, as your husband. I promise to you my love, understanding, and caring, which will allow our love to thrive and grow.

You have, and will have, my support and encouragement. I will be honest with you about my feelings. I will trust you, for without trust we cannot grow together. I promise to respect the qualities that make you the person you are. I will walk with you hand-in-hand, and side-by-side, toward our bright and hopeful future.

ॐॐॐॐॐ

The couple reply "I will" and then add their own words

CELEBRANT

Will you, Carrie, accept Joshua, recognizing that he will grow and change? Will you share his sorrows, and celebrate his triumphs? Will you be honest with him, trust him, respect him, and love him, from this day forward?

BRIDE

I will. Joshua, I promise to support you in everything you do, listen to your opinions and ideas even if I do not agree with them. I promise to walk next to you wherever our future may lead us, to always be there in the good times and the bad times.

I will be your confidante, always by your side, to share your hopes, dreams, and secrets. I will love you and encourage you to achieve all of your goals and dreams, and I want to be there with you when you do achieve them all.

I want our journey to be filled with an enormous amount of love, affection, undying passion, faithfulness, understanding, and an abundance of laughter and fun.

I am so happy and I feel so secure and excited with the idea that you will be my best friend and my one true love for a lifetime.

CELEBRANT

Will you, Joshua, accept Carrie, recognizing that she will grow and change? Will you share her sorrows, and celebrate her triumphs? Will you be honest with her, trust her, respect her, and love her, from this day forward?

GROOM

I will. Carrie, standing before our families and closest friends as witnesses, I promise as your soul mate and husband my heart, support, and love, throughout our lives. As we grow together, have children, and enjoy all the beautiful experiences that marriage offers, I will be the cornerstone, the foundation you can depend on in times of trouble, and the one to rejoice with in times of happiness, for my life will be one with yours.

Know in your heart that I will always love, defend, and put you before anyone else, because I am committed to you for life.

≈≈≈≈≈≈

CELEBRANT

Will you, Peter, take Tama to be your wife, to love and to cherish her through all the days of your life?

GROOM

I will. Tama, from this day forward, I choose you to be my partner in life; to live with you and laugh with you, to stand by your side and sleep in your arms; to be joy to your heart and food to your soul; to bring out the best in you always. For you, I will be the most that I can; and always love you sweetly and gladly, as long as we both shall live.

CELEBRANT

Will you, Tama, take Peter to be your husband, to love and to cherish him through all the days of your life?

BRIDE

I will. Peter, from this day forward, I choose you to be my partner in life; to laugh with you in the good times; to support you in bad times;

to solace you when you are downhearted; to wipe your tears with my hands; to comfort you with my body; to mirror you with my soul; to share with you all my riches and honors; to play with you even when you grow old; and always love you sweetly and gladly, as long as we both shall live.

ॐ ॐ ॐ

ANSWERING "I DO"

CELEBRANT

Linda, do you take this man to be your wedded husband, to share your life with him, and do you pledge that you will love, honor, and care for him in tenderness and affection through all the varying experiences of your lives?

BRIDE

I do.

CELEBRANT

Donald, do you take this woman to be your wedded wife, to share your life with her, and do you pledge that you will love, honor, and care for her, in tenderness and affection through all the varying experiences of your lives?

GROOM

I do.

ॐ ॐ ॐ

ACKNOWLEDGING CHILDREN

GROOM

I, John, do take you, Susan, to be my wife. I acknowledge my love and respect for you and I invite you to share my life as I hope to share yours. I promise to support your dreams and aspirations, and to honor your integrity.

I also promise that I will love and protect your children, Rachel and Scott, and any children we may have together.

BRIDE

I, Susan, do take you, John, to be my husband. I will cherish and protect you, comfort and counsel you, share with you my hopes and worries, my fears and joys, confide in you and trust you, and in all ways consider your physical and emotional well-being.

ॐ ॐ ॐ

REPEATING THE SAME PROMISES

BRIDE

John, I, Denise, will—with great passion and deep affection, be your partner, soulmate and wife. I will be there to comfort and enliven you, to share the blessings and sorrows that our life together may bring. I pledge to you that I will—with your help—be the best mother to our children, and fill our home with discussion, learning, music, creativity, and much love. I salute you, and take you as my intelligent, handsome, sensitive, and sweet husband.

GROOM

Denise, I, John, will—with great passion and deep affection, be your partner, soulmate and husband. I will be there to comfort and enliven you, to share the blessings and sorrows that our life together may bring. I pledge to you that I will—with your help—be the best father to our children, and fill our home with discussion, learning, music, creativity, and much love. I salute you, and take you as my intelligent, beautiful, sensitive, and sweet wife.

ॐॐॐॐॐ

GROOM

I, Paul, do pledge myself to you, Bethany, to love you; to listen as you speak; to speak as you need to hear; to help you fulfill your life as I work to fulfill my own; to work with you to build a home where our hearts may dwell together; to share laughter and tears, dreams and fears; to be faithful during sickness and health, in times of wealth and of want.

I pledge to treat you always with honor and respect, with honesty and patience, as long as we both shall live.

With this ring, I wed myself to you.

BRIDE

I, Bethany, do pledge myself to you, Paul... (repeats above)

Vows in which the couple alternate lines

GROOM

Here in the presence of our family and friends, I promise to be your loving and faithful husband.

BRIDE

And I promise, here in the presence of our family and friends, to be your compassionate and loyal wife.

GROOM

Your love has changed my life. I am a gentler, wiser, and more affectionate person because of you.

BRIDE

Your faith and trust in me has increased my self-assurance and given me great joy.

GROOM

I will do all in my power to nurture our love, to keep it forever as bright as it is in this moment.

BRIDE

I will be true to you and to the love between us for all time.

GROOM

I pledge my love to you.

BRIDE

I pledge my love to you.

Vows in which the couple speak part of their promises in unison

GROOM

I, James, having found with you, Jessica, compatibility and companionship, a spirit of deep and abiding love, a sense of shared values, goals, and purposes so strong and so vital that I want to live my life with you.

I do solemnly accept the duties, obligations and responsibilities of marriage.

I do hereby declare myself to be your husband, to love, honor, and cherish you for the rest of our lives.

BRIDE

I, Jessica, having found with you, James, compatibility and companionship, a spirit of deep and abiding love, a sense of shared values, goals, and purposes so strong and so vital that I want to live my life with you.

I do solemnly accept the duties, obligations and responsibilities of marriage.

I do hereby declare myself to be your wife, to love, honor and cherish you for the rest of our lives.

IN UNISON

I, James/I, Jessica, Do promise to live faithfully together in sympathy and understanding, performing the vows and covenants between us made this date, living according to the ways of truth, beauty, and love, and I do further promise to do all within my power to raise our children to be responsible and productive members of our society and to provide them with an environment conducive to that end.

ॐ ॐ ॐ

VOWS FOR A SECOND MARRIAGE

BRIDE

When I met you my life changed. We have been together for three years and I find that I laugh with joy and delight each day. I risk dreaming of the future, and because you are in my dreams, I do so with pleasure. I look forward to a long and happy life with you, and I promise to care for you and nurture you, and to be your loving wife for the rest of our days.

GROOM

When I met you, I knew immediately that you and I would love each other, but I didn't know that love would heal the wounds I carried with me, and change my life in so many ways. I didn't imagine that I would risk marriage again, but you crept into my heart moment by moment, and tenderness by tenderness. And now, my heart is yours, and I take you for my wife, to love and to cherish, to stand beside you, and support you, forever.

ॐ ॐ ॐ

EXPRESSING PROMISES IN POETRY AND PROSE

GROOM (from Voltaire)

Sensual pleasure passes and vanishes in the twinkling of an eye, but the friendship between us, the mutual confidence, the delights of the heart, the enchantment of the soul, these things do not perish and can never be destroyed. I shall love you until I die.

Janessa, I take you for my wife.

BRIDE *(Sonnet 43, Elizabeth Barrett Browning)*
How do I love thee? Let me count the ways.
I love thee to the depth and breadth and height
My soul can reach, when feeling out of sight
For the ends of Being and ideal Grace.
I love thee to the level of everyday's
Most quiet need, by sun and candlelight.
I love thee freely, as men strive for Right;
I love thee purely, as they turn from Praise.
I love thee with the passion put to use
In my old griefs, and with my childhood's faith.
I love thee with a love I seemed to lose
With my lost saints,—I love thee with the breath,

Smiles, tears, of all my life!—and, if God choose,
I shall but love thee better after death.

Tomás, I take you for my husband.

༄ ༄ ༄ ༄ ༄

CELEBRANT

Stanley and Stephanie will now exchange their vows using the words of Shakespeare's *Sonnet 116.*

BRIDE

Let me not to the marriage of true minds
Admit impediments. Love is not love
Which alters when it alteration finds,
Or bends with the remover to remove:

GROOM

O no! it is an ever-fixèd mark,
That looks on tempests and is never shaken;
It is the star to every wandering bark,
Whose worth's unknown, although his height be taken.

BRIDE

Love's not Time's fool, though rosy lips and cheeks
Within his bending sickle's compass come;
Love alters not with his brief hours and weeks,
But bears it out even to the edge of doom.

GROOM

If this be error, and upon me prov'd,
I never writ, nor no man ever lov'd.

Stephanie, my love will be an ever-fixèd mark, never to be shaken. I cherish you, and joyfully take you as my beloved wife.

BRIDE

Stanley, I accept you as my husband. My love will not alter. It will last until the end of time. I give to you all I am, and joyfully take you as my beloved husband.

ॐ ॐ ॐ

CREATING VOWS FOR SPECIAL OCCASIONS

Valentine's Day

CELEBRANT

Gregory and Serena, on this day of love and romance, St. Valentine's Day, you have chosen to exchange your marriage vows and pledge yourselves to each other forevermore.

GROOM

Serena, with joy and enthusiasm I offer you my heart. Hold it gently. Delight in the love and affection that accompany it. I give it to you freely as I take you for my wife, and pledge to you my constant love and affection. Each year on Valentine's Day, let us celebrate the day we gave our hearts to each other.

BRIDE

Gregory, I take you for my husband, to love and to cherish from one Valentine's Day to another, forever and forever. I give you my heart to love and to cherish as only you know how, and I accept your heart to nourish and hold gently.

A Thanksgiving Day Renewal of Vows

CELEBRANT (*Psalm 100,* adapted by Stephen Mitchell)

Isabella and Antonio come before us this Thanksgiving Day to recommit to their vows of marriage. They were married in this same setting twenty-five years ago on Thanksgiving Day. Before they take their vows, let us offer a prayer of thanksgiving.

Sing to the Lord, all creatures!
Worship him with your joy;
praise him with the sound of your laughter.
Know that we all belong to him,
that he is our source and our home.

Enter his light with thanksgiving;
fill your hearts with his praise.
For his goodness is beyond comprehension,
and his deep love endures forever.

Antonio, please speak your vows to Serena.

GROOM

I, Antonio, renew my vow to cherish, respect, love, and honor you, Serena, for now and forever. I would not trade the life we have had together, for it has brought me a precious friendship and deep and abiding love. On this Thanksgiving Day, I give thanks to you for all the joy you have brought into my life. I thank you for your understanding and support, for the dinners you have cooked, and the children you have raised. In appreciation, I give you this token of my love. (*Places silver necklace around Serena's neck and kisses her.*)

BRIDE

Thank you my love. I, too, have had a rich, loving and supportive relationship these last twenty-five years. With each other's help, we have created a home that is stable, cheerful, and snug. We have raised four fine children together, and we have stayed close friends and loving partners. On this Thanksgiving Day, I feel deep gratitude for the life we have shared together. I love you deeply, and I joyfully renew my marriage vows.

✥✥✥✥✥✥

'Tis not the many oaths that make the truth;
But the plain single vow, that is vow'd true.
—William Shakespeare

Chapter 7

Designing the Opening of
Your Ceremony

That Love is all there is,
Is all we know of Love...
—Emily Dickinson

The opening of the ceremony typically includes a processional, music, a welcome, and a statement of intent.

To start the ceremony, a number of things have to happen. The guests must assemble. The celebrant, the couple, and the rest of the wedding party must be ready to move to their appointed places. The musicians need to know when to begin playing. Someone has to give the signal for everything to start.

༈ ༈ ༈

Deciding How to Begin

The following questions will help you decide how to start your ceremony.

1. *How will your guests know that the ceremony is about to begin?*

   Who will direct them to their places? If you have a limited number of guests gathering in a small area, this can be accomplished by the sound of music, by the bridal party taking their places, or by the celebrant calling them to order. However, if there are many guests or a more formal setting, the ushers should escort them or ask them to take their seats.

2. *How do you want to start your ceremony? Will there be a processional?*

   You don't need a formal setting or a central aisle to have a processional. We've done beautiful weddings in forests, meadows, and backyards, where the members of the wedding created their own aisle amidst the trees and wild flowers. In a restaurant, the couple can wind their way among the tables; in a living room the couple can create the illusion of an aisle by simply walking to the front of the room, parting the guests as they go.

   A processional, however, is not essential. In many weddings, the members of the wedding party informally take their places, and the wedding begins. If you choose not to have a processional, give special consideration to how all of you will get to your places.

3. *What role will music play in this part of your ceremony?*

   Music enriches any wedding. Whether you have a large or small guest list, a formal or informal setting, music can add joy and depth to your ceremony. It can welcome your guests, capture their attention, and set the mood. Music may be playing while your guests gather, or it may start as the celebrant takes his or her place. It may accompany the wedding party as they gather for the ceremony, or as they walk down the aisle. A special piece may announce that the bride or the couple is about to enter. Live music is a special treat, and a friend who will sing or play for you adds personal significance. If live music is not available or is too expensive, music on CD or tape will do just as well. We even did one wedding where the guests were asked to hum "Here Comes the Bride" as the ceremony began!

Don't limit yourselves when making your choices about musical selections. There is an extensive amount of music you can choose from, including classical, pop, rock, country, folk—whatever style you both like best. You have far more choices than the traditional "Wedding March" by Wagner. (See our suggestions in chapter 12.)

A couple of cautions: Long musical selections played while everyone is standing can be uncomfortable. People tend to get restless, they don't know where to look, and they may feel awkward. Music played as background while someone is talking may make it hard to understand the spoken words.

4. What do you want said in the opening?

You can welcome your guests, state the purpose of the gathering, make a statement of philosophy about marriage, have an invocation or a blessing. The opening can be short and informal, or quite formal and substantive. As you discuss this section, keep in mind the mood you want to create.

5. Who will make the opening statement?

Usually it's the celebrant, but it can be one of the attendants, a friend, or parent, or the couple—one or both of them. The size, formality, and setting of your wedding, as well as the mood you want to create, will influence your choice. A welcome by the bride and groom is personal and intimate; by the celebrant, a welcome is more ceremonial or solemn; by the best man or maid of honor it can feel friendly; by a parent it can be very moving.

☙ ☙ ☙

Examples of Openings

SECULAR OPENINGS

Opening for an informal outdoor wedding

The wedding party and the celebrant gather informally, and stand quietly in the midst of a beautiful meadow. Their guests are not far away, talking and visiting with each other. As the wedding party stands waiting, the guests begin to notice and turn their attention to the ceremony. After a few moments, the celebrant speaks to those guests who have not yet quieted and asks for their attention. Then the ceremony begins.

CELEBRANT

Today we celebrate the marriage of John Smith and Mary Wang. Mary and John have asked me to express their love for all of you, and especially to express their deep appreciation to those who have traveled great distances to be here.

Let us all join together, in this beautiful place, breathing the air that connects each of us with every living thing. Let us be silent together, and consider the joy and courage that this man and this woman are demonstrating today, reminding each of us that there is, indeed, life-changing love in our imperfect world. (*Moment of silence.*)

Opening with chimes and guitar

The celebrant and groom are in their places on a cliff overlooking the sea. Chimes sound. Then a guitar plays the processional music. The bridesmaids and groomsmen enter as couples and walk down the path to their places. Again the chime sounds and the bride appears and is accompanied down the path by her brother.

FRIEND

Dwelling in the present moment, I breathe in and calm my body. I breathe out and smile. This is a wonderful moment!

CELEBRANT

Let us join in peace to celebrate the deep love and devotion between Brooke and Hugh.

ᴣᴣᴣᴣᴣᴣᴣᴣ

Opening with a welcome by the family

Musical prelude. Celebrant enters. Processional music: "Kiss to Build a Dream On." The wedding party walks two by two down the aisle. After a pause, the couple enters together and walks down the aisle arm in arm.

CELEBRANT

Edith and Bernie want to warmly welcome you—their families and friends—to share and celebrate their decision to live the rest of their lives together as husband and wife. They take their commitment to each other both seriously and with great joy. Today, they happily proclaim their love to each other, to all of you, and to the world.

BRIDE

Bernie and I are overjoyed to see so many familiar and dear faces with us in this beautiful place. It was important to us to make this a relatively small gathering so we can savor the presence of each one of you. This day is a rite of passage into the strange and wonderful world of wedded life and we will need each one of you to help us navigate in this new world. We cannot thank you enough for being here for us.

CELEBRANT

Who has raised this bride, and is willing to bless and support this union? Who offers this couple their good will and accepts Bernie as a member of their family, granting him their love and affection?

PARENTS OF THE BRIDE

We do. We welcome Bernie into our family.

CELEBRANT

Who has raised this groom, and is willing to bless and support this union? Who offers this couple their good will and accepts Edith as a member of their family, granting her their love and affection?

GROOM'S MOTHER

I do. I welcome Edith into our family.

Bernie and Edith present flowers to their parents.

అప్అప్అప్అప్అప్

Opening for an informal ceremony

The wedding takes place in the family living room. Guests, couple, attendants and celebrant mingle until the celebrant calls for their attention.

CELEBRANT

Let us make a wedding!

We are gathered here together to witness the marriage of Will and Susan. Will and Susan have found in each other a spirit of joy and a sense of companionship, shared purposes, and a love so strong and vital that they wish to combine their lives in marriage.

We join them in that celebration in a spirit of joy.

GROOM

Welcome, friends. Susan and I have asked you here today to witness our wedding. You are our friends and relatives and we want you here with us on this momentous day.

We wrote this ceremony. The words express our thoughts. We know that marriage is not an act to be taken lightly, but is a solemn decision.

We have the determination to make our marriage work. We will bring love, creativity, joy, and even, perhaps, anger and sadness, to each other. We ask of you that you share your lives and your wisdom with us through all our years, our joys, and our tribulations.

BRIDE

To all the friends and family here today: I want to thank you for being there when I needed you, and for giving me strength and guidance.

Today I take Will as my wedded husband, to join him in matrimony. Now the place that was once empty beside me is filled with love. May that love continue to grow and may it touch all those we encounter in the days to come.

ॐॐॐॐॐ

Opening that acknowledges family

BRIDE OR GROOM

Welcome! We have asked you together to witness our marriage and celebrate with us our joy and happiness.

CELEBRANT

We are gathered here to join in the union of two worlds, two worlds that have chanced to cross in the space of one lifetime. And in this lifetime the combined forces of love and respect will guide this new world of oneness into graceful age and eternity: never demanding, or taking from each other, but giving without measure, building a life, sharing all joy and all sadness together.

BRIDE

We now ask you, our family, our friends, to witness this union.

GROOM

To our fathers, the strength of family life, we thank you for showing us right from wrong.

BRIDE

To our mothers, the heart of our families, we thank you for teaching us how to love and to nurture.

GROOM

To all our friends, who helped make us what we are today, we ask you to join with our family to witness our marriage.

Opening for a ceremony of commitment

After the wedding party has informally gathered, the couple welcomes their guests.

PARTNER 1

We have asked you to come together to witness our commitment ceremony and to celebrate with us our love and the joining of our lives.

PARTNER 2

We enter into this union eagerly and with a profound sense of joy. By formalizing our commitment to each other, Chris and I anticipate an enlargement of our lives, even as we have already found our circle of interests and friends enriched and expanded. The delight and approval all of you have expressed so warmly has greatly increased our happiness.

RELIGIOUS OPENINGS

Opening for a large formal ceremony

Celebrant is in place. The string quartet begins playing and the vocalist sings an aria from "Tosca."

The ceremony begins with the ushers entering. The groom walks down the aisle, accompanied by his parents. The bridesmaids follow. Then come the ring bearer and the flower girl. The matron of honor is next. As the bride enters accompanied by her parents, the guests all rise to watch her proceed down the aisle to greet her groom. As the groom comes forward to meet her and walk with her to the altar, the parents step back and take their seats.

CELEBRANT

Let us join in love to celebrate the marriage of Amii and Michael.

Let us pray: God of all people, we rejoice in your presence in the midst of our lives. Grant us the loving hope each of us wishes for Amii and Michael. We praise you for your presence with us, especially in this act of the sacred covenant between them that we are about to witness. Amen. (*Moment of silence.*)

Opening for an interfaith wedding

CELEBRANT

Today, as we joyfully witness the marriage of Tony and Megan, we are also witness to the joining of two distinct religious traditions.

In the beginning, God created design and meaning from the chaotic void. In marriage—a ritual sacred to both Christians and Jews—two people unite in love, and create a new design and meaning for their lives. Megan and Tony both believe in the power and goodness of God. They want their marriage to harmoniously acknowledge and honor the different traditions from which they come.

We celebrate with Tony and Megan their deeply felt similarities, and we participate with them in inventing new ways to bring accord and peace into our world. Together we celebrate the blessing—the shalom—of all creation in the glory of the Lord.

ふふふふふ

Music is well said to be the speech of angels.
—Thomas Carlyle

Chapter 8

Developing the Celebrant's Address

*A successful marriage is an edifice
that must be rebuilt every day.*

—André Maurois

The celebrant is the representative of the state, the community, and sometimes the church. The celebrant's discourse offers a unique opportunity to provide substance and meaning to the ceremony. Depending upon the religion or beliefs of the couple and the celebrant, the address may include an invocation or blessing, a homily, marital advice to the couple, good wishes, or a discourse on the philosophy of marriage.

Usually the statement by the celebrant comes just after the opening. It can be before or after the statements of appreciation by the bride and groom. While the address is not a necessary part of the ceremony, it is customary. Your desires, the kind of ceremony you are having, as well as the celebrant's philosophy or religious requirements determine what the celebrant will say. You'll probably find that you don't have to write this section; most celebrants prefer to write their own. Don't hesitate to let your celebrant know if there are particular ideas or selections you want included— or excluded.

This address requires special attention by couples who have nontraditional philosophical or religious beliefs, who are marrying across ethnic or religious lines, or who have strong feelings about what they do and do not want said in their ceremony. Take the time early in the planning process to discuss your needs thoroughly with the celebrant to make sure that there are no conflicts or surprises.

ॐ ॐ ॐ

Sample Addresses by the Celebrant

SECULAR COMMENTS ON LOVE AND MARRIAGE

Advice to the couple

CELEBRANT

This marriage will be a celebration of all the mystery and wonder that deep love brings to living.

I encourage you both to preserve and renew this marriage, to keep fully alive, to grow, to change, to maintain your capacity for wonder and for spontaneity, to remain flexible, warm, and sensitive to each other. Give time to each other, no matter what demands are made upon your day. Nurture each other to fullness and wholeness, realizing that each of you will need, at times, to bring strength and support to each other. I encourage you, as you grow to love each other more deeply, to discover out of this love a larger love for all of creation.

ॐॐॐॐॐ

Marriage as a miracle

CELEBRANT

Charles and Joanne, you have inspired and transformed each other with the vision of your future together. You both treasure integrity, peacefulness, and a sense of celebration of life. You find each other generous, gentle, bright, and loyal. You both love travel, appreciate a shared sense of humor, and together, you honor and cherish the idea of family.

We are asking you, Charles and Joanne, to perform a miracle—which is what a good marriage really is. A miracle, and nothing less. For this marriage brings together two people, each brought up in different households, with different traditions and experiences. Now we ask you, different persons that you are, to respond fully to each other with enduring love. We expect you to continue to grow—both as individuals and as a couple—for the rest of your lives, and, as you grow to still see each other as agreeable, admirable, and supportive. At the core of every successful marriage are care and concern, giving and sharing, a strength and intimacy that accepts the other exactly as she or he is.

We know inside what we intend to say, but we do not always know what the other person hears. Sometimes communication will be difficult; some misunderstandings are inevitable. Give each other the benefit of the doubt: Learn to listen to the music, not just the words.

Love

CELEBRANT

To love devotedly means to grow in consciousness. Love breathes more deeply as we develop awareness. At the core of such awareness are care and concern, giving and sharing, a strength and intimacy that leaves no room for fear or distrust.

To love devotedly requires honesty. Being true to oneself means being true to the other. Chris and Dale have found in each other someone with whom to be honest, with whom to be at ease, with whom to be at home. In this extraordinary setting at the edge of the sea, surrounded by friends and families, we are reminded that the boundaries that separate us are also the places where we meet. The powerful sound of the waves beneath us and the beautiful, age-old cypress trees around us, inspire with their life and natural beauty. Your relationship abounds with good will; and while you differ from one another, you have found you value many of the same things— your ability to communicate, your shared spiritual journey, and your mutual desire to live each moment fully.

Marriage creates the security for two people to fully open themselves to each other. Within the safety of this commitment you will create the opportunity to accept another person as a complete being—one who experiences both hopes and fears, satisfaction and suffering. Marriage provides a relationship in which you can have and be a lover, an ally, and a partner. And it is only through this commitment that you can discover true intimacy—in which hidden and protected parts of yourselves are permitted to come forth, find acceptance, and help you become whole. The strength this brings enables each of you to open more readily to the world, beginning an unending cycle of reciprocity.

ぞぞぞぞぞ

The nature of marriage

CELEBRANT

A wedding is a time for sharing with friends and family the joyfulness of a new phase in the relationship of two people. Linda and Art have invited us here tonight to share in their joy and celebrate their wedding with them.

Marriage is a commitment to a relationship. It is a commitment to do everything possible to keep that relationship growing and dynamic. However, if the relationship between two people does not already exist, this ceremony will not create it.

As you, Linda and Art, publicly announce the existence of the bond uniting you, keep in mind that you—not a celebrant, not the state— created this marriage.

You have agreed to make a commitment to each other and announce it publicly. Although you recognize that no one person can ever fulfill all your human needs, you have turned to marriage now in order to advance your relationship.

ぞぞぞぞぞ

The meaning of marriage

CELEBRANT

What is the meaning of marriage? Essentially the word denotes union, the intertwining of the lives of a man and a woman, socially, physically, materially, and emotionally. However, no matter how idyllic the courtship, no marriage attains immediate fulfillment. You know that as there are no perfect joys, so there are no absolute sorrows. In the sharing of your problems, in your adjustments to one another, you are strengthening your marriage. However, remember that it is no more realistic to expect perfection from your partner than to expect it from yourself.

Each of you brings to the other and to this union the experiences of your lives with your own families. The importance of those experiences—your appreciation of human differences, your own hopes and fears, and the strength that arises from mutual respect, understanding and love—will all contribute to the strength of your marriage as your life together unfolds.

You must never forget that you are individuals, and that there can be mutual respect only so long as the individuality of each of you remains important to both of you. While you will have pride in each other's achievements, while you will offer each to the other every help, encouragement and support, remember that you have neither merged nor submerged your identities.

As the poet Gibran says, "Let there be spaces in your togetherness."[1]

A Humanist address

CELEBRANT

Marriage is a sharing of experience and an adventure in the most intimate of human relationships. It is the joyous union of two individuals whose companionship and mutual understanding have flowered into romance. Today as James and Pamela proclaim their love to the world, we who are gathered here rejoice with them and for them in the new life they now undertake together.

This wedding in the humanist spirit celebrates the joy and the beauty of life. In Humanism, reason is the guide, but reason never separated from the emotions and strivings of the whole person. Humanism celebrates emotion and intellect functioning together to provide the firmest foundation for married love.

Marriage must be a cooperative venture in every sense. It is a relationship based on love, respect, and a determination on the part of both wife and husband to adjust to each other's temperaments and moods — in health or sickness, joy or sadness, ease or hardship. In love, the paradox occurs that two beings become one and yet remain two.

ॐॐॐॐॐ

Words for a reaffirmation ceremony

CELEBRANT *(Notes on Love and Courage,* Hugh Prather)
the quiet thoughts
of two people a long time in love
touch lightly
like birds nesting in each other's warmth
you will know them by their laughter
but to each other
they speak mostly through their solitude
if they find themselves apart
they may dream of sitting undisturbed
in each other's presence
of wrapping themselves warmly
in each other's ease

ॐ ॐ ॐ

RELIGIOUS REFLECTIONS ON LOVE AND MARRIAGE

CELEBRANT *(On Marriage,* Joseph Campbell)
It is not surprising that in the New Testament the first miracle of Jesus is set at a wedding, in Cana. There Jesus transmutes water into wine: the flat necessity of life into the spirited, Dionysian, active substance of spirit.

All marriages take place in Cana, for in all marriages the necessary raw material of life—water—is changed into a sparkling, tingling, inspiriting element of the soul: wine.

It is entirely appropriate that at weddings and at renewals of vows, couples celebrate the union of their lives and the qualities of their souls with traditional prayers, poetry, wine and ritual action.

Marriage is holy not only because it is a precious and revered way of forming human lives, but also because it is a form of religion in itself, a special way in which spirituality pours into life.

There's no need, of course, to think about myth, theology, and alchemy in order to live the miracle of marriage. One need only enter into it fully and tend its soul, of whatever kind and in whatever direction it leads, even into darkness.

Marriage is by nature miraculous and magical. We do not understand it, and cannot know where it is headed. To care for its soul, it is more important to honor its mystery than to try to outwit its intentions for what we, with our small minds, may think is a better outcome.

If you want to ensure the soulfulness of your marriage, it would be infinitely better to build a shrine to it, find its god or goddess and tend its image, than to follow the "manual" and do it all properly and intelligently.

For all of us, of whatever religion or nonreligion, a marriage is a sacrament. To care for its soul we need to be priests rather than technicians, and to draw from the wellspring of ordinary piety, rather than from theory or formula.[2]

Emphasis on commitment

CELEBRANT

Terri and Michael, your marriage is intended to join you for life in a relationship so intimate and personal that it will change your whole being. It offers you the hope of a love that is true and mature. To attain such love, you will have to commit yourselves to one another, freely, gladly, and completely, for the sake of a deeper and richer life together. Let God be your guide and helper as you find the strength to live your lives together with courage.

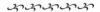

The meaning of Islamic marriage

CELEBRANT

Islamic marriage is a serious, mutual commitment of two people, before Allah as their witness, to achieve mutual love and kindness, truthfulness and straightforwardness. Muslim marriage is the most intimate relationship.

Since perfection belongs to Allah alone, marriage requires an appreciation and tolerance of human shortcomings. Marriage also requires mutual respect, complimenting each other in the presence of others; mutual protection of the interests of each other; faithfulness and loyalty to each other.

The main purposes of Islamic marriage are pleasure to Allah; physical, mental, and spiritual peace and tranquility; continuation of the human race; and permanent, healthy, and holy companionship.

This marriage calls on you both to act righteously, as such behavior will carry you into everlasting life.

An interfaith wedding with both a priest and a rabbi as celebrants

PRIEST

We are here to celebrate the joining of two different traditions that have in common a reverence for Almighty God.

RABBI

The boundaries that separate us are also the places where we meet. The two of you—in joining your lives—bring together two distinct heritages, but your love and high regard for each other will be the cement that binds these building blocks together in a strong foundation. By this marriage, you are demonstrating that ancient hostilities between Christians and Jews need not persist.

PRIEST

The weaving together of your different traditions does not require that you abandon the rich religions of each of your upbringings. It is your common faith in the God of us all that can guide you in the path of righteousness, as you construct and preserve a strong and moral marriage. Let your differences instruct and enrich each of you. Let us pray.

RABBI

Blessed are you, Unnameable God, source of the universe, who purifies us with your commandments and gives us marriage as a path to you.

PRIEST

Father, by your power you gave man the constant help of woman so that man and woman should no longer be two, but one flesh. We honor your teaching that what you have united may not be divided.

RABBI

Blessed are you, Unnameable God, source of the universe, creator of woman and man in your image. Give joy to these two loving friends, as you gave joy to the first man and woman in the Garden of Eden. Blessed are you, Unnameable God, who gives joy to this bride and groom.

PRIEST

Give them the strength that comes from your Holy Scripture; keep them always true to your commandments so that they may set an example of trust, love, and peace.

☙☙☙☙☙

Love is like quicksilver in the hand.
Leave the fingers open and it stays.
Clutch it, and it darts away.

—Dorothy Parker

Chapter 9

Choosing the Rituals for Your Ceremony

Love doesn't just sit there, like a stone;
it has to be made, like bread,
remade all the time, made new.

— Ursula K. LeGuin

Add depth, excitement, and meaning to your ceremony through the use of ritual. Adapt, innovate, devise, create, and mold the old, the new, the religious, the spiritual, and the secular. In choosing rituals, you can turn to traditional religion, your ethnic background, other world cultures, or you can allow your imagination to run free.

The most common ritual in a wedding is the giving or exchanging of rings as a token symbolizing your commitments. Single and double ring ceremonies are both common. Some couples prefer to use a variation on this theme—the exchange of some other type of jewelry or token of love. The ring ritual usually follows the vows.

The second most common ritual is a variant of a wine (or water, or juice) ritual. There are as many different interpretations of this ritual as there are different cultures. You may toast each other, share from one cup, symbolize your individuality by sipping from different cups, or each sip from the glass and then break it.

There are many other rituals that can be used in addition to, or instead of, the ring and wine ceremonies.

Ethnic traditions are the source of many rituals. Look to your own ethnic heritage, or others you admire, to find exciting options. Or use your creativity to invent a ritual that has special meaning for the two of you.

Couples also create rites from personally significant symbols and events. Some examples:

- Baking a loaf of bread together and sharing it with guests, representing the importance of community
- Distributing flowers to guests as a gift of beauty and love
- Using candles to create a mood of peace and serenity during a midnight ceremony
- Releasing doves or butterflies or bubbles at the end of the ceremony to signify freedom and joy
- Standing within a circle formed by guests, symbolic of closeness and intimacy with family and friends

Rituals offer a wonderful opportunity for creativity. In addition to the ideas you'll find here, consider creating rituals using incense, meditation, chanting, or responsive readings. Every aspect of the ceremony can have symbolic value if you are willing to pay attention to details and trust your own inventiveness.

࿐ ࿐ ࿐

A Variety of Rituals

RING RITUALS

Traditional words

With this ring, I thee wed.

࿐࿐࿐࿐࿐

Single ring ceremonies

CELEBRANT

Say what is in your heart as you share the ring.

GROOM *(turns to best man and takes the ring)*

Candace, you are my beloved. You are my friend. I take you for my wife.

৵৵৵৵৵

CELEBRANT

The wedding ring is a sacred symbol encircling the finger, which many ancient people believed contained a vein running directly to the heart. It not only represents the physical connecting of these two; it also reflects the cosmic bond that joins them.

Walter, please place the ring on Joanna's finger.

GROOM

Joanna, with this ring I marry you and join my life with yours.

৵৵৵৵৵

Double ring ceremonies

CELEBRANT *(takes the rings from the best man and matron of honor and holds them aloft)*

The circle is the symbol of the sun, of the moon, and of the universe. It is the symbol of wholeness, of perfection, and of peace. These rings are the symbol of unity in which your two lives are now joined in one unbroken circle of love.

The celebrant hands the bride's ring to the groom. The bride hands her bouquet to her matron of honor and gives her left hand to her groom.

GROOM

Karen, I give you this ring, not as jewelry, but as a part of me; not to encircle just your finger, but your whole being. In doing this, I take you as my wife. (*Places wedding band on ring finger of her left hand.*)

The celebrant hands the groom's ring to the bride. She takes her groom's left hand.

BRIDE

James, I have chosen this ring. As I put it on your finger, I take you as my husband. May our love continue as endlessly as this circle of gold. (*Places wedding band on ring finger of his left hand.*)

ᘯᘯᘯᘯᘯ

CELEBRANT

Rings are an ancient symbol, blessed and simple. Circles—for love that is given comes back around. Round like the sun, like a perfect pearl, like arms that embrace. Therefore, may these symbols remind you that your love, like the sun, illuminates; that your love, like the pearl, grows in luster; and that your love, like arms that embrace, is a grace upon this world. May you wear them in peace and deepening love.

GROOM

Deborah, I give you this ring as a symbol of my love for you, my covenant to be your husband, and to be faithful to you.

With this ring, I thee wed. (*Jerome places the ring on Deborah's finger.*)

BRIDE

Jerome, I give you this ring as a symbol of my love for you, my covenant to be your wife, and to be faithful to you.

With this ring, I thee wed. (*Deborah places the ring on Jerome's finger.*)

ᘯᘯᘯᘯᘯ

A religious ring ritual: Repeat after me

CELEBRANT

Bless, O Lord, the giving of these rings that they who wear them may abide in thy peace, and continue in thy favor.

The precious nature of your rings represents the subtle and wonderful essence you find by losing yourselves in each other, and the subtle and wonderful essence you find individually, through your mutual love, respect and support. Now let us witness the sealing of your promises with these rings, sign and token of the world the two of you will create from this day forth.

Sally, please repeat after me: Marvin, I give you this ring,

BRIDE

Marvin, I give you this ring,

CELEBRANT

in token of the covenant made between us this day,

BRIDE

in token of the covenant made between us this day,

CELEBRANT

in the sight of God.

BRIDE

in the sight of God.

CELEBRANT *(repeats the above words for the groom)*

Marvin, please repeat after me. Sally, I give you this ring....

ॐ ॐ ॐ

WINE RITUALS

Sipping from two glasses

CELEBRANT *(pours wine into two goblets and then holds up both glasses)*

We bless this wine. May the sharing of this cup symbolize the sharing of your life together, giving to each other and receiving from each other, with enthusiasm and delight. *(Hands the glasses to the couple.)*

GROOM *(toasting his partner)*

Let this wine represent the spirit of life. By drinking this wine now, we show our desire to blend our spirits together making our union stronger. I drink with you to our marriage! *(Both drink.)*

BRIDE *(toasting her partner)*

Let this wine represent the joy and richness of life. By drinking this wine now, we show our determination to bring sweetness and love to our union. I drink with you to our marriage! *(Both drink. The two exchange glasses and sip again.)*

BOTH *(toasting each other)*

To our love and our marriage.

The wedding guests participate in the wine ritual

Following the drinking by the couple, the best man takes the glasses and speaks to the guests.

BEST MAN

Wine is a product of the earth, the rain, and the sun. As they are one, so are we all one. Pat and Tom invite you to share with them in their celebration by taking a sip of wine and passing it on. *(Hands glasses to nearby guests. They sip, and pass them on. Or tiny cups of wine can be distributed and the guests can all toast the couple.)*

Sweet and tart wines

CELEBRANT *(Pours tart wine into one of two glasses.)*

To symbolize your life together, I invite you to sip this tart wine to remind you of the difficult times you will encounter. *(Hands glass to the groom, who sips and passes the glass to the bride. She also sips, and returns the glass to the celebrant, who pours sweet wine into the second glass.)*

Now please sip this sweet wine to symbolize the richness of overcoming trying times. *(Repeats process.)*

Breaking the wine glass

GROOM

An ancient custom is to break the goblet after we share the wine. Drinking the wine reminds us of the great joys that lie ahead; the breaking of the goblet signifies the sorrows we may have to endure. The broken glass also symbolizes the uniqueness of this moment, for only our lips touch this goblet—no others ever will.

Bride and groom sip. The best man then wraps the glass in a napkin or puts it in a special cloth bag, and the groom crushes the glass under his heel.

Returning wine to the earth

CELEBRANT

Nancy and Al, drink from this one glass as a symbol of your sharing of life. (*The bride and groom each sip from the glass.*)

Now give the remaining wine back to the earth as a reminder that what nourishes us must also be nourished. (*The groom pours the remainder of the wine on the ground.*)

Break the glass as a recognition of the evanescence of life—and as a letting go of the past, living in the present, and looking toward the future. (*The bride wraps the glass in a napkin, hands it to the groom and he crushes it with his foot.*)

Several interpretations of the breaking of the glass

CELEBRANT

Andrew and Denise, having sipped of your wine, only one tradition remains: breaking the wine glasses. A medieval interpretation of this custom has the groom smash the cup against the northern wall, the direction from which the evil spirits were believed to originate. While the demons were busy getting tipsy, the couple would dash off to consummate the marriage so that, in their moment of vulnerability, their love would not be stolen.

Another explanation holds that the drinking of the wine and then the breaking of the glass is to remind you that what matters is the spirit, not the letter; the wine, not the glass. Having two glasses also provides you the opportunity for declaring that each is equal to the other. Andrew and Denise, please join your hands and smash your glasses at the same time. (*Each throws the glass at a large rock several feet away and not near any people.*)

A ritual using wine and water

CELEBRANT

Water and wine represent the moon and the sun, the feminine and the masculine, and all other complementary pairs in the universe. As you, Jim and Pat, share water from the same cup, you drink in the feminine and receptive energies. (*The couple drink from the water cup.*)

As you sip from this wine cup, you drink in the active and masculine energies. (*The couple drink from the wine cup.*)

May this sharing symbolize the sharing of your life together and the enrichment of your worlds as you complement and harmonize with each other.

A ritual using wine and bread

CELEBRANT

Wine is the spirit and celebration of life; bread, the staff of life. Sharing wine and breaking bread together creates a community of caring and belonging. Wendy and Jim now invite you to partake of this bread and wine, in celebration of their union.

The bread and wine are passed. The guests break pieces from the loaf, and dip them in the wine. "All I Ask of You" is played during the ritual.

ॐ ॐ ॐ

RITUALS USING FLOWERS, CANDLES, AND BELLS

A flower ceremony including the guests

CELEBRANT

Now the bride and groom will pass the bridal bouquet among friends and relatives, asking each of you to take one flower. Later, Agnes and Jeff will invite you to cast your flower into the brook, and offer a secret, silent wish for their present and future happiness.

A silent flower ritual honoring the couple's mothers

This lovely and touching flower ritual is most effective when only the bride and the celebrant (and possibly the groom) know about it in advance: When the bride reaches the altar, but before the ceremony begins, she walks to her mother, presenting her with a flower from her bouquet. She then presents one to the groom's mother. She returns to the groom and the ceremony begins.

A Unity candle ceremony

Bride and groom each hold a lighted candle.

CELEBRANT

This is the evening of a beautiful day and the dawning of a new life for Cindy and Chuck.

They come here before you, their loved ones and friends, still as two separate and unique individuals, bringing their own special qualities, talents, and personalities, symbolized by the flame of each separate candle. They choose to be united in marriage. (*The bride and groom move forward and, in unison, light a candle.*)

ぷぷぷぷぷ

Another Unity candle ritual

CELEBRANT

Alexis and Ruth—each of you now take a candle, and with them, light this new, larger candle. This common candle sends forth a single light, formed from the uniqueness and individuality you both bring to this marriage.

I encourage you to take time at your future wedding anniversaries or at other special times to light this candle again, and renew your promises to each other as you grow through the changes of life together.

ぷぷぷぷぷ

A candle ritual with the mothers participating

CELEBRANT

Regina and Ann, as the mothers of this couple—as the ones who gave them life and who nurtured them—Angela and Daniel are grateful to you, and would like you now to light the candles that they will use later in this ceremony as they formally commit themselves to each other.

ぷぷぷぷぷ

Bell ringing ritual by guests

Guests are given small bells. At the end of the ceremony, when the bride and groom kiss, the guests ring the bells vigorously, calling to mind the ringing of church bells.

ETHNIC RITUALS

African-American: Jumping the broom

A resurgence of the search for roots has brought back the tradition of jumping the broom, a ritual that dates back to slave days when legal marriage was forbidden. The universal need for ritual led people to create means by which they could express their innermost dreams and hopes with the materials at hand. In this case, the wedding couple used a brightly decorated broom to sweep out the old and to jump into their new lives.

CELEBRANT *(speaking to a friend of the couple)*
Donna, will you please bring the broom to us? *(While Donna is bringing the broom, celebrant continues.)*

Jumping the broom is an old African tradition. It represents the joining of the couple, the combining of two families, and the need for the community to support the marriage.

This broom has special significance: it belongs to a very special couple—Lysa's grandparents, who are unable to be with us today. It was used to celebrate their fiftieth wedding anniversary. And it was borrowed with the hope and expectation of passing along the longevity of that marriage to Lysa and Mark. For Mark and Lysa, it also demonstrates their determination to leap over any obstacles—together—as they embark upon their future.

Donna brings the broom and places it upon the ground in front of Lysa and Mark. Lysa and Mark join hands, jump over the broom together and kiss.

Celtic: A Scottish procession

In Scotland, the bride is escorted, arms linked, in procession with the bridesmaid on one side, the groomsman on the other. Her two companions each flourish white scarves and handkerchiefs in their hands, waving them about her like fans. At the rear of the bridal procession come two young girls similarly festooned with white scarves while at the procession's fore, pipers play.

Celtic: Handfasting

Handfasting originated in pre-Christian Celtic marriage rituals. In them, the couple's hands were bound to each other ritually for the duration of the ceremony. The original idea behind them was to marry for a fixed amount of time, subject to renewal. Nine years was a very common figure, as was a year and a day, though shorter periods were also known.

Needed for the ritual: a strip of vine, garlands, or silk, for binding the hands of the couple—(a long scarf might be nice here), and gifts to exchange—usually the rings, and a basket with a handle.

In the marriage ceremony, some acknowledgment is made that the physical binding about to take place is symbolic of a greater, cosmic bond. A verbal acknowledgment of the other might be appropriate here. Next, the "receptive" hands of the couple are bound together by the official—the receptive hand is the opposite of the dominant hand. A right-handed person would bind his left hand—though with two left-handed people, custom would dictate binding the right hands. Then a statement is made about the symbolism of joining hands, such as:

"You, and not anyone else but you—in this life, and into the life eternal."

Gifts are then exchanged between them—the wedding rings would work here. Some mention may be made of the wedding ring being a sacred symbol encircling the finger, which many ancient people believed contained a vein running directly to the heart. The ring symbolizes the special protection given to the bearer and to the couple, a symbol of their vow of honor to uphold the handfasting oath just taken. Other vows of any type may follow the handfasting oath. A wine ritual, or a ritual involving bread, a kiss, or anything else, can be inserted here.

The "marriage basket" can be hooked over the bound hands of those being joined, or placed elsewhere in the ceremony. It can be offered to them as a wedding present, or the couple can add symbolic items to it during the ceremony, and mix them to symbolize their union.[3]

Chinese: Tea pouring ceremony

In this ritual, a Chinese-American couple wished to honor and pay tribute to their parents. They wished symbolically to acknowledge that, with their marriage, they had attained the status of being able to care for their parents, instead of being taken care of by them.

The rite of passage they designed took place immediately after the celebrant had asked each set of parents whether they accepted their new child-in-law as a beloved member of the family.

CELEBRANT

In recognition of Jennifer's Chinese heritage, Scott and Jennifer now reenact an ancient ritual in which they show their deep respect and gratitude to their parents by serving tea to them.

In addition to demonstrating their esteem and affection by this act, it also represents the establishment of their own household, where their parents will always be welcomed with honor and hospitality.

The couple, in a slow, deliberate choreography, set beautiful teacups before each parent. The groom lifts the teapot, hands it to the bride, and she carefully pours some tea into each cup.

When all have been served, each parent in turn lifts the cup, nods to the bride and groom, and then sips from the cup.

The ritual takes place in total silence. After the fourth parent has sipped, the wedding ceremony continues.

Guatemalan: Wedding chain

A beautifully wrought silver Guatemalan wedding chain had been in the family of the groom for many generations. During the ceremony, the couples' mothers ceremonially draped the chain over the shoulders of the bride and groom, symbolizing the bond that connected them.

ॐॐॐॐॐ

Eastern European: Crowning

Many variations of crowning and coronation occur in Eastern Orthodox and Coptic weddings. The priest will exchange crowns between the bride and groom three times. The couple may circle the altar three times. The rings may also be exchanged three times, or the couple may light three candles that are tied together, or be asked three times if they consent to marry.

Hindu: The seven steps

CELEBRANT

Renuka and Matthew now introduce us to a contemporary version of the ancient Hindu ritual of seven steps—satapadi. Originally, the bride and groom together circled a fire seven times, each time touching a sanctified stone spread with sandalwood oil. Today, Renuka and Matthew will alternate reciting the seven steps.

GROOM

Let us take the first step,
to provide for our household a nourishing and pure diet,
avoiding those foods injurious to healthy living.

BRIDE

Let us take the second step,
to develop physical, mental, and spiritual powers.

GROOM

Let us take the third step,
to increase our wealth by righteous means and proper use.

BRIDE

Let us take the fourth step,
to acquire knowledge, happiness, and harmony by mutual love and trust.

GROOM

Let us take the fifth step,
so that we will be blessed with strong, virtuous, and heroic children.

BRIDE

Let us take the sixth step,
for self-restraint and longevity.

GROOM

Finally, let us take the seventh step,
to be true companions and remain lifelong partners by this wedlock.

BRIDE

We have taken the Seven Steps.
You have become mine forever.

GROOM

Yes, we have become partners
I have become yours.
Hereafter, I cannot live without you.
Do not live without me.

BRIDE

Let us share the joys.
We are word and meaning, united.
You are thought and I am sound.

GROOM

May the earth be honey-sweet for us.
May the heavens be honey-sweet for us.

BRIDE

May the plants be honey-sweet for us.
May the sun be all honey for us.
May the cows yield us honey-sweet milk!

GROOM

As the heavens are stable,
As the earth is stable,
As the mountains are stable,
as the whole universe is stable,
so may our union be permanently settled.[4]

ﭢﭢﭢﭢﭢ

Iranian: *The bounty of the earth*

CELEBRANT

From the Persian traditions of Ali's family, we have before us this beautifully arranged table, with colorful flowers, fruit, vegetables, and honey—the bounty of our fertile earth.

It has been lovingly put together and arranged by Ali's mother, Parivash, his aunt Azar and his sister Azita.

This colorful spread of richness represents abundance—a cornucopia of all the good things we wish for this couple in their married life.

It also includes a mirror, to reflect the joy of this moment of commitment, and to preserve the significant image of the bonding of Adele and Ali; this mirror will become a permanent part of their household.

Now, from an ancient Iranian tradition, Adele and Ali symbolize the sharing of their lives, and the nurturing of each other, by feeding each other from the honey bowl. (*Each dips a pinkie into the bowl of honey and feeds the other.*)

ﭢﭢﭢﭢﭢ

Japanese: *Sansankudo—a sake ritual*

CELEBRANT

From the most ancient of times, drinking from the same cup has symbolized the strongest of bonds into which two persons can enter: a powerful symbol of agreement, of affection, and of peace. Sipping from the same cup symbolizes the life the couple will share, each giving to the other generously and freely, each receiving from the other fully. This venerable tradition is common to many cultures.

The Japanese version of this ritual is called sansankudo, which means three times three or nine, and signifies the concept of forever. Hikado and Audrey have adapted this ancient ritual for their wedding. On the table before us are three vessels of increasing size. I will pour three portions of sake into each cup, and Audrey and Hikado will each sip three times from each cup. May the sharing of these cups symbolize the sharing of your life together.

The three wine cups are nested one inside the other. The celebrant pours three portions of sake from an okoshi into the smallest cup. The groom takes the cup, holds it for the bride who sips three times. She then holds it while the groom sips three times. The celebrant pours sake into the next larger cup, and the couple repeats the ritual. Again, the celebrant pours sake into the largest cup, and the couple drinks again. All is done silently.[5]

Jewish: The chuppah

CELEBRANT

We are holding this celebration underneath a canopy, called a chuppah. Chuppah literally means "that which covers, or floats above."

In Jewish custom, the chuppah is the house of promises; it is the home of hope. It represents the new home which the bride and groom are creating today. The fact that the chuppah is open on all sides represents the ideal of hospitality: visitors will always know that this new home is open, ready to welcome them as honored guests.

The chuppah is not a very strong structure, it needs loving friends and family to hold it up, and this fact, too, is symbolic, for the real value of a home is not its framework: its real value lies with the people who are in it, who love and choose to be together, to be a family.

Jewish: The breaking of the wine glass

CELEBRANT

To conclude our ceremony we again borrow from Jewish custom: the breaking of the wine glass. The shattering of this glass symbolizes that what matters most in life is the spirit, not the letter—the contents, not the cup. It also represents the uniqueness of the moment, for only Sarah and Aaron will sip from this glass—no others ever will.

It signifies that this act of commitment can never be undone, and it ensures that this glass will never be used for anything less important than this marriage of Sarah and Aaron.

The smashing of this glass tells us that our joy in this union is so great that no vessel can contain it.

As Aaron now breaks this glass, let us all join in and rejoice with the sound of celebration!

Tibetan: Chiming bowl

The celebrant strikes a Tibetan chiming bowl and waits for the sound to diminish. The bride and groom each light a taper, then together light a larger candle. When the larger flame is established, the celebrant strikes the chiming bowl again.

I would like to have engraved inside every wedding band: Be kind to one another. This is the Golden Rule of marriage and the secret of making love last through the years.

—Randolph Ray

Chapter 10

Involving Family

The family is one of nature's masterpieces.
—George Santayana

A warm, personal way to honor your families and other important people is to include them in your ceremony.

Don't limit yourself to such obvious traditions as Dad accompanying the bride down the aisle, Sis serving as matron of honor, or nephew as ring bearer. Some ethnic groups have a far richer variety that you can adapt. This is your chance to innovate—to create a ritual of your own that will make your wedding special.

There's no one place to include family members; they can be involved in any ritual in any part of the ceremony.

ॐ ॐ ॐ

Choosing Rituals for Family Members

Whom would you like to honor? You may include grandparents, parents, siblings, children, or other beloved relatives or friends, to conduct part of the ceremony, welcome their new son or daughter, read a poem, give a blessing, sign the wedding license, participate as a member of the bridal party, or take part in any other ritual. (You may also choose to acknowledge others who are not present, or who are deceased.)

If you already have children, acknowledging them in the ceremony is a lovely way to welcome them into your newly fashioned family. You can invent an appropriate way to include a child of any age.

Consider including other young children in the ceremony, such as nieces, nephews, cousins, or the offspring of friends. They can participate in the ceremony as ring bearers, flower girls or boys, pages, junior bridesmaids, or ushers. Or they can be great helpers by soliciting signatures for the guest book, or distributing programs or favors.

Engage your creative energy and imagination.

ॐ ॐ ॐ

A Selection of Family Participation Rituals

INVOLVING PARENTS, GRANDPARENTS, AND OTHER ADULTS

On __not__ giving away the bride

CELEBRANT
  Who gives this woman to be married?

PARENT OR FRIEND
  No one gives her; no one can. She gives herself.

Welcome by the family

CELEBRANT
  Who is it who welcomes Victor as a grandson, loving friend, and husband of Diane?

BRIDE'S GRANDPARENTS
  We do.

GROOM *(to the grandparents)*

Otto and Mae, this marriage brings me into your lives in a new and special way. I hope our friendship and affection for each other will be greater because of it.

CELEBRANT

Who is it who welcomes Diane as a daughter, loving friend, and wife of Victor?

GROOM'S MOTHER

I do.

BRIDE *(to the groom's mother)*

Margaret, this marriage brings into your life three people who already love you. You are a grandmother and mother-in-law all at one time. Please know that we value our loving friendship with you and look forward to sharing this special relationship with you.

Father's statement of support for a same-sex couple

Lisa and Jane, your marriage signals a new phase in your relationship. It also signals to parents to stand aside and let the two of you face life's challenges together: making decisions, solving problems, and in all other ways seeking your own happiness. As parents, we love and enjoy you both. I know I speak for both families in wishing you both happiness and good fortune in your marriage.

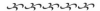

The parents escort the couple to the altar

Nancy's parents accompanied her to the altar, while Al's mother accompanied him. Their families joined them as a symbol of the love and sustenance they have shared.

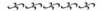

Acknowledging family members who are not present

CELEBRANT

We want to acknowledge those people who are so important to Kyle and Kristen who are not able to be here with us today. Some, like Kyle's grandfather, are too ill to travel. Others are no longer with us, especially Kristen's grandmother and grandfather. They are here in spirit and in our hearts.

A flower ritual to honor family members

CELEBRANT

Colleen and Heinz come together today to create a new family. Colleen now gives white roses to her grandfather and her grandmother, James and Marie, as a symbol of her enduring love, gratitude and deep respect. (*Colleen walks to her grandparents, takes two white roses from her bouquet, and presents each one with a flower. She then returns to her place beside Heinz.*)

Heinz and Colleen also have roses for their mothers to thank them for their continuing love and support. (*The maid of honor translates the celebrant's comments into German. Colleen and Heinz walk first to Colleen's mother and then to Heinz's mother, presenting each with a flower.*)

ॐ ॐ ॐ

INVOLVING CHILDREN

Statement to the children of a previous marriage

BRIDE (*to the groom's son*)

Charles, since I met your father, we have grown together to become a family. Each of us has gained a new awareness of the others' needs and rights. Thank you for the joy, satisfaction, and love you have given me.

GROOM *(to the bride's daughter)*

Karen, your mother and I will continue to respect you as an individual. I love you dearly, and promise to be there for you always.

సైసైసైసైసై

A gift-giving ritual to acknowledge a young child

CELEBRANT

Do you, Amy, love James and want him to marry your mother and be your father?

CHILD

I do.

CELEBRANT

Do you, James and Phoebe, promise to provide Amy with a loving home?

BRIDE AND GROOM

We do.

GROOM *(to stepdaughter)*

Amy, I love your Mommy and I love you dearly as well. I want to be a second father to you and I look forward to many happy times as a new family.

Please wear this necklace to remember this special day. (*He places the necklace around Amy's neck.*)

సైసైసైసైసై

Statement by older children

DAUGHTER

Clarence, for the past two years you have been both my friend and my father. I love you and I want to be the first to welcome you into our family.

SON

Clarence, you are more of a father than my birth father, and I love you. This marriage will be good, not only for you and Mom, but for us also. I welcome you with all my heart.

སྐྲ་སྐྲ་སྐྲ་སྐྲ་སྐྲ་

A flower ritual including several children

CELEBRANT

Mary Jo and Tim, the two of you are combining your strengths and hopes in this marriage. Your decision to marry will also shape and deeply affect the lives of Jennifer, Heather, Erin, and Brian. The six of you will touch each other in a special way from now on. Today we are acknowledging both the creation of a marriage and the creation of a family.

Each of you will contribute your individual blossoms to this new entity, combining your special selves into a bouquet that is more rich and varied than any of you could create by yourselves. I ask you now to symbolize the wonder and beauty of the birth of this new family by each offering your flower to create a single bouquet. (*Each puts a flower into the vase.*)

YOUNGEST CHILD

Together our new family will be happy.

སྐྲ་སྐྲ་སྐྲ་སྐྲ་སྐྲ་

*Children in a family
are like flowers in a bouquet:
there's always one determined
to face in an opposite direction
from the way the arranger desires.*

—Marcelene Cox

Chapter 11

Closing Your Ceremony

This is the miracle that happens every time
to those who really love:
the more they give, the more they possess.
—Rainer Maria Rilke

Ceremonies usually close with the kiss, the pronouncement that the couple is now married, a benediction or good wishes, music, and a recessional.

How you handle the closing will determine whether the ceremony comes to a smooth conclusion or just fizzles out, leaving people confused and uncomfortable. If your ceremony is not traditional, your guests may not know what you expect them to do. This is less of a problem in ceremonies that end with a recessional, but because many contemporary ceremonies don't, your careful attention is necessary. Music is frequently used in the closing to provide a definitive conclusion to the event.

In thinking about the closing, consider the location, whether there is a central aisle, and whether or not there will be music and a recessional.

The celebrant typically speaks the closing words, but they can be said by the bride, the groom, the best man or maid of honor, or another person.

ৡ ৡ ৡ

Deciding How to End

1. *Will you include the ritual kiss? Do you want a pronouncement that you are now partners for life?*

The kiss is usually the climax of the ceremony. A pronouncement signifies the legal fulfillment of the wedding ceremony. Traditionally the celebrant says, "I now pronounce you husband and wife," but there are many other ways to phrase the pronouncement. You may even choose to pronounce *yourselves* legally married.

2. *Do you want a benediction or good wishes as part of the closing?*

A benediction in a religious context, or good wishes in a secular one, is a blessing of the couple, and sometimes of the guests. The benediction may precede or follow the kiss.

3. *Will you have a recessional?*

You don't have to have a recessional just because you had a processional. And you may have a recessional even if you didn't have a processional. Guests usually follow the bridal party out, thus clearly marking the closing of the ceremony. However, such conventional ways of dealing with the closing may not work for you. If your ceremony is in an informal setting, you may want just to turn and greet your guests, breaking ranks and signaling to everyone that the ceremony is over.

4. *Will you have music to mark the end of the ceremony?*

If so, it should be a cheerful, triumphant, and bright selection, reflecting the joyousness of your marriage. See chapter 12 for suggestions.

5. *Will you have a receiving line?*

A receiving line usually follows a very formal ceremony. However, if you plan to have a great many guests, consider the discomfort of having to stand in one place with a continuous smile as each guest greets you. An alternative is for the newlyweds to circulate among their guests during the reception.

If you choose to have a receiving line, who will be in the line? Where will you stand to receive your guests? Will it immediately follow the ceremony? Will you have the line in the place where the ceremony took place or at the reception? Do you want your guests to follow the recessional to find the line? If you delay the receiving line until later, how will your guests know where and when? What will they do in the meantime?

৯ৎ ৯ৎ ৯ৎ

A Medley of Closings

A Nonsectarian Religious Closing

Couple exchange rings.

CELEBRANT *(to the guests)*
Let us pray. *(All recite the Lord's Prayer or another of your choice.)*

May God be with you and help you to grow together. May the Lord bless and keep you. May the Lord cause his face to shine upon you and be gracious unto you. May the Lord lift his countenance upon you and give you peace. Amen.

(To the couple) By virtue of the authority vested in me, and in conformity with the laws of the State of New Jersey, I now pronounce you, Nathaniel, and you, Sarah, husband and wife. As you bow your heads, I invoke God's blessing upon you. May you enjoy the peace of home, of mind, and of heart.

Nathaniel and Sarah, you may now kiss. (*Bride and groom kiss. The couple turn to their guests and are greeted with hugs and best wishes by their parents and friends.*)

ॐ ॐ ॐ

SECULAR CLOSING

Closing with a flower ritual

(Couple exchange rings.)

CELEBRANT (*to the guests*)

We know not what the future may bring into the life of this couple, but we hope that together they may be equal to the needs of their tomorrows. May they find in all times an ever-growing love.

Shelli and Keith treasure the wisdom and seek the blessings of you who are gathered here. They seek your support and love to see them through the life adventure ahead.

(*To the couple*) Keith and Shelli, you have formalized in our presence the existence of the bond already between you, vowing to be loyal and loving toward one another. In expressing your private affirmations, you have pronounced yourselves husband and wife.

We celebrate the love that has brought you to this moment. May your joy deepen with the passing years as you explore the mystery and meaning of your love.

We wish for you a home that is a haven from the turmoil of the world, a place of harmony and peace, security and strength, life and laughter. Trusting each other, may you trust life, and never be afraid. May the affection and joy you share radiate, enriching the lives of your families, your friends, and all others whom you touch.

It is now my privilege to present you with your first gifts as a married couple. From medieval times, the rose has been a symbol of love. (*Gives each of them a rose.*)

Please exchange your roses now, giving each other the gift of love and beauty. (*They exchange roses.*)

As your life together unfolds, frequently renew your commitment to each other with gifts of roses.

From this moment on, venture your separate ways together, remembering always to be each other's best and truest friend. Go in peace. Live simply, live gently. Be just in your words and deeds. Let not the demands of this marriage eclipse the friends who have sustained you.

Crave peace for all the peoples of the world, beginning with yourselves. With abiding confidence and affection, we send you forth upon your journey in life together.

(To guests) I call on all of you to witness that Shelli and Keith have exchanged their vows in our presence, and according to the laws of the State of California they are now husband and wife.

(To couple) You may now kiss each other for the first time as a married couple. (*Bride and groom kiss.*)

(To guests) Shelli and Keith will spend the first few moments of their marriage by themselves. Please make your way to the garden and enjoy some refreshment. They will rejoin you in a little while.

(Music trio: Recessional.)

ॐ ॐ ॐ

BENEDICTIONS AND GOOD WISHES

Traditional Irish blessing

May the road rise to meet you
May the wind be ever at your back
May the good Lord ever keep you
In the hollow of His hand
May your hearts be warm as your hearthstone
And may God bless you always.

ॐॐॐॐॐ

Unitarian benediction

May the God you worship be a blessing and a support to your lives.
May the God you honor help make your lives gracious and good.
May the God you serve be a light in your lives and bring you peace.

ౢౢౢౢౢ

Good Wishes

CELEBRANT

We share with Kirk and Jenny their happiness. May they bring their best to their marriage.

Thus shall their contentment be made lasting, and they will be truly united, not merely by the form and words of this ceremony, but by their hopes and joys, their sharing of the burdens life will bring, and by the happy and mysterious merging of their spirits.

May love bless this union, and make its days constantly increase in joy and satisfaction.

ౢౢౢౢౢ

More Good Wishes

CELEBRANT *(to the guests)*

Audrey and Paul have opened the door to comradeship and mystery, growth and fulfillment. What will the future bring them? We cannot say. We can only wish them the best life has to offer. May they bring intelligence as well as faith to the task that is set before them. May they maintain enduring trust and respect for one another. May they find patience in times of stress, strength in times of frailty, courage in times of difficulty, vision in times of doubt, and in all times, an ever-growing love. Audrey and Paul ask you who are gathered here to give them your blessings.

Best wishes for the couple with a response by the guests

CELEBRANT *(to the guests)*

We know not what the future may bring into the lives of this couple, but we pray that together they may be equal to the needs of their tomorrows. I ask all of you who have heard the promises Anita and Zachary have made to each other, will each of you promise to do everything in your power to support them, their commitment, and their marriage? If so, respond by saying, "I will."

GUESTS

I will!

ॐ ॐ ॐ

PRONOUNCEMENTS AND THE KISS

Secular

CELEBRANT *(to the guests)*

Jana and Lowell, having found in one another a spirit of deep and abiding love, and being willing to accept the duties, obligations and responsibilities to each other, to their children, and to our society, which are inherent in a marriage contract, I do hereby declare them to be husband and wife, each to love, honor and cherish the other for the rest of their lives.

Bride and groom turn to each other and kiss. Their attendants offer best wishes and hugs, followed by their parents, and then their guests.

ॐॐॐॐॐ

Religious

CELEBRANT

Kyle and Kirsten, as mortal beings, with human strengths and weaknesses, you stand today, and promise faith. You will find your faith as you live, each moment consecrated to truth, and to a good whose presence you have deeply felt. Now, from this time forward, love the love in you that underlies your love. With each other, share your wonder at the beauty that you find in each other. As we end this ceremony, begin your new life in the company of those you love.

I call on all of you to witness that Kirsten and Kyle have exchanged their vows, in the presence of God and this company, and according the laws of the State of California, they are now husband and wife. Kirsten, Kyle, you may now kiss each other for the first time as a married couple! (*Bride and groom kiss.*)

Joyous recessional music plays. The couple walk up the aisle, followed by their attendants and the celebrant. The guests follow.

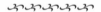

Pronouncement and best wishes

CELEBRANT

Bill and Teri have pledged themselves to each other in the presence of this company, and I do now pronounce them husband and wife. May we all join with them in a commitment to make this a world of peace, a world of comradeship, a world without prejudice, a world of friends undivided by creed or class, a world in which children can live out their lives untouched by war or poverty, fear or hate. May all that is noble, lovely and true abide with you forever. (*Bride and groom kiss.*)

Best man and maid of honor give hugs and kisses; parents and friends follow them.

Pronouncement, best wishes and injunction

CELEBRANT

In as much as Gary and Linda have consented together in this ceremony to live in wedlock, and have stated their vows in the presence of this company and before these witnesses, and before me, as a representative of the community, I call upon all here to recognize that they are now husband and wife. Linda, you may kiss your groom! (*Couple kisses. Guests applaud.*)

To Gary and Linda, may I extend my best wishes for your continued happiness, today and all the days of your lives. May I ask you both to abide in your dedication, as expressed by the prophet Micah, "To do justice and love mercy..."

I propose that we now all toast the bride and groom: To long life and happiness. May the cup of your lives be full of sweetness.

જ્જ્જ્જ્જ્

All weddings are happy. It's trying to live together afterwards that causes all the problems.
—Shelley Winters (adapted)

Chapter 12

Including Poetry, Prose, Music, and More

Read from some humble poet,
Whose songs gushed from his heart,
As showers from the clouds of summer,
Or tears from the eyelids start.

—Henry W. Longfellow

Enrich your ceremony with the beauty and grandeur of poetry and music. Readings, music, recollections and good wishes may be offered as *gifts* to the couple during the ceremony. Music adds meaning and warmth and is a perfect accompaniment to some rituals. Our greatest writers, poets and composers provide you with expressions of ideals, love, commitment and marriage.

Sometimes, symbolically important gifts are incorporated into the ceremony. For example, in one wedding, friends presented the couple with a home-baked loaf of bread for a bread-sharing ritual. In another, for the wine ritual, the best man presented wine bottled in the year the couple met. Such presentations may be made immediately after the introduction or anywhere else during the ceremony that seems appropriate.

Ask the special people in your life to be a part of your wedding. If you have a friend who is a talented musician or singer, you may want to invite that person to sing or play. If you want poetry as part of the ceremony, ask a member of your wedding party or another special friend to read something, perhaps even something they themselves have written. If you want a toast made during the ceremony, invite your guests to offer their thoughts, feelings, and wishes for you.

Do you have a favorite poem, song, or story? It could be something well known, such as Elizabeth Barrett Browning's "How Do I Love Thee," or Shakespeare's "Sonnet 116"—*Let me not to the marriage of true minds admit impediments.* It could be something from your religious heritage, such as a passage from Song of Songs or First Corinthians. It could be a favorite ballad such as "Our Love is Here to Stay." A reading from *The Velveteen Rabbit* or "The Owl and The Pussycat" can add a touch of humor or inspiration. Or you can choose something that has special meaning for you, such as "Desiderata" or the words of a favorite popular song (with or without music). The possibilities are limitless.

You may want to choose the specific poetry, music, or sentiment, or leave the choice up to the reader.

If your ceremony is secular but your parents want some traditional religious elements, a beautiful reading from the Bible or an inspiring piece of music may help meet their needs without compromising yours.

We offer a selection of poetry, readings and musical selections below. There are also many anthologies and resource lists available to help you choose poetry and music. See your local librarian and our suggestions in chapter 17.

ॐ ॐ ॐ

A Selection of Poetry

CLASSICAL POETRY

A Lover and His Lass, William Shakespeare

>It was a lover and his lass
>>With a hey and a ho, and a hey-nonino!
>That o'er the green cornfield did pass

In the spring time, the only pretty ring time,
When birds do sing hey ding a ding ding:
   Sweet lovers love the Spring.

Between the acres of the rye
   With a hey and a ho, and a hey-nonino!
These pretty country folks would lie:
   In the spring time, the only pretty ring time,
When birds do sing hey ding a ding ding:
   Sweet lovers love the Spring.

This carol they began that hour,
   With a hey and a ho, and a hey-nonino!
How that a life was but a flower:
   In the spring time, the only pretty ring time,
When birds do sing hey ding a ding ding:
   Sweet lovers love the Spring.

And therefore take the present time
   With a hey and a ho, and a hey-nonino!
For love is crownèd with the prime
   In spring time, the only pretty ring time,
When birds do sing hey ding a ding ding:
   Sweet lovers love the Spring.

ॐॐॐॐॐ

The Passionate Shepherd to His Love, Christopher Marlowe

Come live with me and be my Love,
And we will all the pleasures prove
That hills and valleys, dales and field
And all the craggy mountains yield.

There will we sit upon the rocks
And see the shepherds feed their flocks,
By shallow rivers to whose falls
Melodious birds sing madrigals.

And I will make thee beds of roses
With a thousand fragrant posies,
A cap of flowers and a kirtle
Embroidered all with leaves of myrtle.

A gown made of the finest wool,
Which from our pretty lambs we pull,
Fair-linèd slippers for the cold,
With buckles of the purest gold.

A belt of straw and ivy buds
With coral clasps and amber studs:
And if these pleasures may thee move,
Come live with me and be my Love.

The silver dishes for the meat
As precious as the gods do eat,
Shall on an ivory table be
Prepared each day for thee and me.

The shepherds' swains shall dance and sing
For thy delight each May-morning:
If these delights thy mind may move,
Then live with me and be my Love.

ॐॐॐॐॐ

Love's Philosophy, Percy Bysshe Shelley

The fountains mingle with the river
    And the rivers with the ocean,
The winds of heaven mix for ever
    With a sweet emotion;
Nothing in the world is single,
    All things by a law divine
In one another's being mingle—
    Why not I with thine?

See the mountains kiss high heaven
    And the waves clasp one another;
No sister-flower would be forgiven

If it disdain'd its brother:
And the sunlight clasps the earth,
    And the moonbeams kiss the sea—
What are all these kissings worth,
    If thou kiss not me?

చి౩చి౩చి౩

My True Love Hath My Heart, **Sir Philip Sidney**

My true-love hath my heart, and I have his,
By just exchange one for another given;
I hold his dear, and mine he cannot miss,
There never was a better bargain driven:
    My true-love hath my heart, and I have his.

His heart in me keeps him and me in one,
My heart in him his thoughts and senses guides;
He loves my heart, for once it was his own,
I cherish his because in me it bides:
    My true-love hath my heart, and I have his.

చి౩చి౩చి౩

The Birthday, **Christina Rossetti**

My heart is like a singing bird
    Whose nest is in a watered shoot;
My heart is like an apple tree
    Whose boughs are bent with thick-set fruit;
My heart is like a rainbow shell
    That paddles in a halcyon sea;
My heart is gladder than all these
    Because my love is come to me.

Raise me a dais of silk and down;
    Hang it with vair and purple dyes;
Carve it in doves and pomegranates,
    And peacocks with a hundred eyes;

Work it in gold and silver grapes,
   In leaves and silver fleur-de-lys;
Because the birthday of my life
Is come, my love is come to me.

ゐゐゐゐゐ

The First Day, Christina Rossetti

I wish I could remember the first day,
First hour, first moment of your meeting me;
If bright or dim the season, it might be
Summer or winter for aught I can say.
So unrecorded did it slip away,
So blind was I to see and to foresee,
So dull to mark the budding of my tree
That would not blossom yet for many a May.
If only I could recollect it! Such
A day of days! I let it come and go
As traceless as a thaw of bygone snow.
It seemed to mean so little, meant so much!
If only now I could recall that touch,
First touch of hand in hand!—Did one but know!

ॐ ॐ ॐ

MODERN POETRY

love is more thicker than forget, e e cummings

love is more thicker than forget
more thinner than recall
more seldom than a wave is wet
more frequent than to fail

it is most mad and moonly
and less it shall unbe
than all the sea which only
is deeper than the sea

love is less always than to win
less never than alive
less bigger than the least begin
less littler than forgive

it is most sane and sunly
and more it cannot die
than all the sky which only
is higher than the sky

ॐॐॐॐॐ

Excerpt from *Song of the Open Road,* Walt Whitman

Listen! I will be honest with you,
I do not offer the old smooth prizes, but offer rough
    new prizes,
These are the days that must happen to you:
You shall not heap up what is call'd riches,
You shall scatter with lavish hand all that you earn
    or achieve,
You but arrive at the city to which you were
    destin'd, you hardly settle yourself to satisfac-
    tion before you are call'd by an irresistible call
    to depart,
You shall be treated to the ironical smiles and
    mockings of those who remain behind you,
What beckonings of love you receive you shall only
    answer with passionate kisses of parting,
You shall not allow the hold of those who spread
    their reach'd hands toward you.

Allons! the road is before us!
It is safe—I have tried it—my own feet have tried it
    well—be not detain'd!
Let the paper remain on the desk unwritten, and the
    book on the shelf unopen'd!
Let the tools remain in the workshop! let the money
    remain unearn'd!

Let the school stand! mind not the cry of the teacher!
Let the preacher preach in his pulpit! let the lawyer plead in the court, and the judge expound the law.

Camerado, I give you my hand!
I give you my love more precious than money,
I give you myself before preaching or law;
Will you give me yourself? will you come travel with me?
Shall we stick by each other as long as we live?

I Saw in Louisiana a Live-Oak Growing, **Walt Whitman**

I saw in Louisiana a live-oak growing,
All alone stood it and the moss hung down from the branches,
Without any companion it grew there uttering joyous leaves of dark green,
And its look, rude, unbending, lusty, made me think of myself,
But I wonder'd how it could utter joyous leaves standing alone there without its friend near, for I knew I could not,
And I broke off a twig with a certain number of leaves upon it, and twined around it a little moss,
And brought it away, and I have placed it in sight, in my room,
It is not needed to remind me as of my own dear friends,
(For I believe lately I think of little else than of them,)
Yet it remains to me a curious token, it makes me think of manly love;

For all that, and though the live-oak glistens there in
    Louisiana solitary in a wide flat space,
Uttering joyous leaves all its life without a friend, a
    lover near,
I know very well I could not.

☙☙☙☙☙

The Minute I Heard My First Love Story, Rumi

The minute I heard my first love story
I started looking for you, not knowing
how blind that was.

Lovers don't finally meet somewhere.
They're in each other all along.

☙☙☙☙☙

June 17, 1846, on the North Platte, Ruth Whitman

This morning is fierce with fresh smells:
prairie grass   clover   and the familiar
lupin paler than the sky bluer
than the periwinkle starring the ground
around the stream under willows and alders

I pick the wild blossom and mark the joining
of leaf to stem the design of
petal to petal
          and I remember
the kiss of fingers
the joining   the holiday of eyes
in an Illinois meadow
        I had brought my class
        to study the wildflowers
        not knowing the tall farmer watching us
        owned the field and would be my future
        refuge

a widow of thirty five I had thought
my body would not stir again
my lifelong fires were banked
but in his rich earth
winter buds unclenched their tightness
under his sun   his unaccustomed rain
I shed my widowhood
and let a new self burgeon

husbanded again have I finally learned
to let be let go? the need
to find oneself within a man
is not so great the second time

but we are like two voices of a strain
that come together and go apart
each echoing but singing independently
knowing the coming together in the end
        will thread into a single theme

ॐ ॐ ॐ

LIGHTHEARTED POETRY

Romance, Robert Louis Stevenson

I will make you brooches and toys for your delight
Of bird-song at morning and star-shine at night.
I will make a palace fit for you and me,
Of green days in forests and blue days at sea.

I will make my kitchen, and you shall keep your room
Where white flows the river and bright blows the broom,
And you shall wash your linen and keep your body white
In rainfall at morning and dewfall at night.

And this shall be for music when no one else is near,
The fine song for singing, the rare song to hear!
That only I remember, that only you admire,
Of the broad road that stretches and the roadside fire.

Love Song, **Gloria Elizabeth**

> If I had a mouthful of kisses,
> I would scatter them over your face,
>   like little white flowers.
>
> Had I a heartful of love,
> I would pour it over your body,
>   like spring water pure and clear.
>
> If I had a soulful of fears,
> I would deliver them over to you,
>   gold sovereigns from a secret hoard.
>
> I have a mouthful,
> a heartful,
> a soulful.
>
> Please take them.

Love in the Middle of the Air, **Lenore Kandel**

> CATCH ME!
>   I love you, I trust you,
>   I love you
> CATCH ME!
>   catch my left foot, my right
>   foot, my hand!
>   here I am hanging by my teeth
>   300 feet up in the air and
> CATCH ME!
>   here I come, flying without wings,
>   no parachute, doing a double triple
>   super flip-flop somersault
>   RIGHT UP HERE WITHOUT A
>   SAFETY NET AND
> CATCH ME!

you caught me!
I love you!
now it's *your* turn

ॐ ॐ ॐ

Readings from the Bible

From *First Letter to the Corinthians*

If I have the gift of prophecy, and can fathom all mysteries and all knowledge, and if I have a faith that can move mountains, but have not love, I am nothing. If I give all that I possess to the poor, and surrender my body to the flames, but have not love, I gain nothing.

Love is patient, love is kind. It does not envy, it does not boast, it is not proud. It is not rude, it is not selfish. It is not easily angered, it keeps no record of wrongs. Love does not delight in evil, but rejoices with the truth. Love protects all things, has faith in all things, hopes for all things, endures all things.

The gifts of prophecy will in time fail; and knowledge too will vanish away. But love does not come to an end. Know you, then, that there are three things that last: Faith, Hope and Love. And the greatest of these is Love. And the greatest of these is Love.

Psalm I, adapted by Stephen Mitchell

Blessed are the man and the woman
    who have grown beyond themselves
    and have seen through their separations.
They delight in the way things are
    and keep their hearts open, day and night.
They are like trees planted near flowing rivers,
    which bear fruit when they are ready.
Their leaves will not fall or wither.
    Everything they do will succeed.

ॐॐॐॐॐॐ

From the Greek Orthodox marriage service

Be thou magnified, O bridegroom, like Abraham, and blessed like Isaac, and increase like Jacob, walking in peace and living in righteousness...

And thou, O bride, be magnified like Sarah, and rejoice like Rebecca, and increase like Rachel, being glad in thy husband and keeping the bounds of the law...[6]

ॐॐॐॐॐ

Excerpts from *Song of Songs*

Come then, my love;
   my darling, come with me.
The winter is over; the rains
   have stopped;
   in the countryside the
   flowers are in bloom,
This is the time for singing;
   the song of doves is heard in
   the fields.
Figs are beginning to ripen;
   the air is fragrant with
   blossoming vines.
Come then, my love;
   my darling, come with me.

My sweetheart, my bride, is a
   secret garden,
a walled garden, a private
   spring;
   there the plants flourish.
They grow like an orchard of
   pomegranate trees
   and bear the finest fruits.
There is no lack of henna and
   nard,

of saffron, calamus, and
    cinnamon,
or incense of every kind.
Myrrh and aloes grow there
    with all the most fragrant
        perfumes.
Fountains water the garden,
    streams of flowing water,
    brooks gushing down from
        the Lebanon Mountains.

Under the apple tree I woke you,
    in the place where you were
        born.
Close your heart to every love
    but mine;
    hold no one in your arms
    but me.
Love is as powerful as death;
    passion is as strong as death
        itself.
It bursts into flame
    and burns like a raging fire.
Water cannot put it out;
    no flood can drown it.
But if anyone tried to buy love
    with his wealth,
    contempt is all he would get.

ॐ ॐ ॐ

Prose Selections

From *Letters to a Young Poet,* Rainer Maria Rilke

For one human being to love another human being: that is perhaps the most difficult task that has been entrusted to us, the ultimate task, the final test and proof, the work for which all other work is merely preparation. Loving does not at first mean merging, surrendering, and uniting with another person—it is a high inducement for the individual to ripen, to become something in himself, to become world, to become world in himself for the sake of another person; it is a great, demanding claim on him, something that chooses him and calls him to vast distances.

ॐॐॐॐॐ

From *Poetry and Marriage,* Wendell Berry

The meaning of marriage begins in the giving of words. We cannot join ourselves to one another without giving our word. And this must be an unconditional giving, for in joining ourselves to one another we join ourselves to the unknown. We can join one another only by joining the unknown. We must not be misled by the procedures of experimental thought: in life, in the world, we are never given two known results to choose between, but only one result that we choose without knowing what it is.

Marriage rests upon the immutable givens that compose it: words, bodies, characters, histories, places. Some wishes cannot succeed; some victories cannot be won; some loneliness is incorrigible. But there is relief and freedom in knowing what is real; these givens come to us out of the perennial reality of the world, like the terrain we live on. One does not care for this ground to make it a different place, or to make it perfect, but to make it inhabitable and to make it better. To flee from its realities is only to arrive at them unprepared.

Because the condition of marriage is worldly and its meaning communal, no one party to it can be solely in charge. What you alone think it ought to be, it is not going to be. Where you alone think you want it to go, it is not going to go. It is going where the two of you—and marriage, time, life, history, and the world—will take it. You do not know the road; you have committed your life to a way.

ᢌᢌᢌᢌᢌᢌ

From *The Imitation of Christ,* Thomas à Kempis

Love is a great thing, a great good in every way; it alone lightens what is heavy, and leads smoothly over all roughness. For it carries a burden without being burdened, and makes every bitter thing sweet and tasty. Love wants to be lifted up, not held back by anything low. Love wants to be free, and far from all worldly desires, so that its inner vision may not be dimmed and good fortune bind it or misfortune cast it down. Nothing is sweeter than love; nothing stronger, nothing higher, nothing wider; nothing happier, nothing fuller, nothing better in heaven and earth; for love is born of God, and can find rest only in God, beyond all created things.

Love flies, runs, and rejoices; it is free and nothing can hold it back. It gives all for all, and has all in all, because it rests in the highest good, from whom all goodness originates and flows. It doesn't look to the gifts, but to the giver of all good things. Love often knows no limits, but burns beyond every limit. Love feels no burden, shrinks from no effort, aims beyond its strength, sees nothing as impossible, for it believes that all things are possible and allowable to it. Thus it is capable of everything, and it succeeds because it is confident of the result, while someone without love loses courage and gives up.

ᢌᢌᢌᢌᢌᢌ

Charles Dickens

We're too old to be single. Why shouldn't we both be married instead of sitting through the long winter evenings by our solitary firesides? Why shouldn't we make one fireside of it?

Come, let's be a comfortable couple and take care of each other! How glad we shall be, that we have somebody we are fond of always, to talk to and sit with.

Let's be a comfortable couple. Now do, my dear![7]

ॐॐॐॐॐ

From *A Gift from the Sea,* Anne Morrow Lindbergh

When you love someone, you do not love them all the time, in exactly the same way from moment to moment. It is an impossibility. It is even a lie to pretend to. And yet this is exactly what most of us demand. We have so little faith in the ebb and flow of life, of love, of relationships. We leap at the flow of the tide and resist in terror its ebb. We are afraid it will never return. We insist on permanency, on duration, on continuity; when the only continuity possible, in life as in love, is in growth, in fluidity—in freedom, in the sense that the dancers are free, barely touching as they pass, but partners in the same pattern. The only real security is not in owning or possessing, not in demanding or expecting, not in hoping, even. Security in a relationship lies neither in looking back to what it was in nostalgia, nor forward to what it might be in dread or anticipation, but living in the present relationship and accepting it as it is now. For relationships, too, must be like islands. One must accept them for what they are here and now, within their limits—islands, surrounded and interrupted by the sea, continually visited and abandoned by the tides. One must accept the security of the wingèd life, of ebb and flow, of intermittency.

ॐ ॐ ॐ

Readings from Different Cultures

FROM THE CHINESE TRADITION

From *The Importance of Living,* Lin Yutang

Lin Yutang tells us:

> ...the analogy of clay and water in human marriage was long ago expressed by Madame Kuan, wife of the great Yüan painter Chao Mengfu and herself a painter and teacher at the Imperial Court. When in their middle age Chao's ardor was cooling, or anyway when he was thinking of taking a mistress, Madame Kuan wrote the following poem, which touched his heart and changed his mind:

'Twixt You and Me, Kuan Tao-Sheng

'Twixt you and me
There's too much emotion.
That's the reason why
There's such a commotion!
Take a lump of clay,
Wet it, pat it,
And make an image of me,
And an image of you.
Then smash them, crash them,
And add a little water.
Break them and re-make them
Into an image of you,
And an image of me.
Then in my clay, there's a little of you.
And in your clay, there's a little of me.
And nothing ever shall us sever;
Living, we'll sleep in the same quilt,
And dead, we'll be buried together.

ॐ ॐ ॐ

FROM NATIVE AMERICAN TRADITIONS

Hymn to the Sun, Great Plains Indians

O Morning Star! When you look down upon us,
give us peace and refreshing sleep.

Great Spirit! Bless our children, friends
and visitors through a happy life.

May our trails lie straight and level before us.
Let us live to behold.
We are all your children and ask these things with good hearts.

ॐॐॐॐॐ

Prayer to the Four Directions, Blackfoot

To the West:

Over there are the mountains. May you see them as long as you live, for from them you receive sweet pine for incense.

To the North:

Strength will come from the North. May you look for many years upon the star that never moves.

To the East:

Old age will come from below, from where comes the light of the Sun.

To the South:

May warm winds of the South bring you food.

ॐ ॐ ॐ

FROM AFRICAN TRADITIONS

Prayer to the New Moon, African

May you be for us a moon of joy and happiness. Let the young become strong and the grown man maintain his strength, the pregnant woman be delivered and the woman who has given birth, suckle her child. Let the stranger come to the end of his journey and those who remain at home dwell safely in their houses. Let flocks that go to feed in the pastures return happily. May you be a moon of harvest and of calves. May you be a moon of restoration and of good health.

ॐॐॐॐॐ

African Wedding Benediction, Anonymous

Libations! Libations!
To the protective spirits on high!
To the wandering spirits below!
To the spirits of the mountains,

To the spirits of the valleys,
To the spirits of the East,
To the spirits of the West,
To the spirits of the North,
To the spirits of the South,
To the bride and groom, together, libation!

May the spirits on high, as well as the spirits below, fill you with grace!

Divine helpers, come! Keep watch all night! Rather than see the bridegroom so much as damage his toenail, may the good spirits go ahead of him. May the bride not so much as damage her fingernail! The good spirits will be their cushions so that not a hair on their heads shall be harmed.

And you, all you good wedding guests waiting in the shadows, come out into the light! May the light follow you!

ॐ ॐ ॐ

Music

Music has great power to influence the tone of your ceremony. It can generate a range of emotions from joy to sadness; it can inspire serious or celebratory feelings; and it can arouse a sense of triumph or romance.

While tradition holds that the bride enters to the strains of the Wagner wedding march (the "Bridal Chorus" from *Lohengrin*), and that the couple departs to the jubilant sound of Mendelssohn's "Wedding March" (from *Midsummer Night's Dream),* classical music offers an almost endless array of attractive options. In recent years, the *Kanon in D* by Pachelbel has been used extensively as an accompaniment to the processional or recessional.

Other popular selections for the entrance include the "Allegro maestoso" from Handel's *Water Music,* Purcell's *Trumpet Voluntary,* and the "Trio for Two Flutes and Harp" from *L'Enfance du Christ* by Berlioz. Many familiar selections from the works of Bach are also suitable, including "Jesu, Joy of Man's Desiring,"

"Sheep May Safely Graze," "Air for G String," or the "Andante" from his *Brandenburg Concerto No. 2*.

However, classical music is not the only appropriate choice. If the two of you share a love for other types of music, use it to put your personal stamp on the ceremony. We have conducted weddings that featured Dixieland jazz for entrances and exits, popular songs that had special meaning for the couple, original compositions by a composer friend, and ethnic music reflecting the couple's heritage.

Choose music that's personally pleasing; it's your signature on the ceremony.

If you engage professional musicians, audition carefully and select a group that plays the music you like. They can draw on their own repertoire to make suggestions for appropriate pieces. But if you let them select compositions, make sure that it is music both you and your partner really like. Don't hesitate to make special requests.

If you are using recorded accompaniment, take the time to browse and listen to a variety of styles on CD or cassette. The music that frames your ceremony will profoundly effect the mood and feeling of your whole ceremony

A comprehensive list of suitable musical selections would fill hundreds of pages; the following guidelines are intended to stimulate your thinking and steer you toward some options.

ॐ ॐ ॐ

MUSIC FOR THE PRELUDE AND PROCESSIONAL

The music for the prelude is essentially background, as guests gather and take their seats. It should not be intrusive, and it should anticipate the tone and mood of the ceremony to follow.

If you want the processional to express the feeling of a pageant, choose music that is stately, serious, and slow. The classical music catalog abounds with good possibilities: Handel, Mozart, and Haydn, among many others. But we suggest that you also listen attentively to music by composers from the Baroque era such as Corelli, Vivaldi, Boyce; and some from the

Romantic period: Rachmaninoff, Chopin, Tchaikovsky, or Brahms.

If you want suggestions because you don't know anything about classical music, ask a friend who does, call your local library, visit a large record store, or ask someone at a classical music radio station, if your community has one.

For a nostalgic, romantic flavor, don't overlook popular songs or show tunes from the 30s, 40s and 50s. They have particular appeal if you or your guests were around when they were big hits.

ॐ ॐ ॐ

MUSIC DURING THE CEREMONY

Be careful if you plan to use music during the ceremony. An instrumental interlude can feel to your guests like an interruption of the ceremony, or like treading water while they wait for something else to happen. However, if you choose selections that are not distracting, instrumental music—whether live or recorded—can greatly enhance the effect of a candle or wine-sharing ritual.

ॐ ॐ ॐ

MUSIC FOR THE RECESSIONAL

Ending with music for the recessional strengthens the whole ceremony by putting a frame around it. To heighten the feelings of joy and triumph, pick lively, celebratory accompaniment, the kind of music that lifts the heart, brings a smile, and stimulates applause.

Trust your own taste and judgment. It's your wedding, so let the music you choose reflect your personal preferences.

ॐ ॐ ॐ

Good Wishes and Blessings

You can add personal blessings, wishes, benedictions or prayers to any part of your ceremony. They can be offered by the

celebrant, parents, or friends, and including them enriches the
wedding ritual with a warm, serious and optimistic flavor.

READER

We wish for you a life with books and poetry and music and
laughter—a life filled with all the things that represent the highest
strivings of humanity. We hope that your lives stand as a symbol of
human beings living together in love and peace, seeking truth, and
demanding social justice.

ᔐᔐᔐᔐᔐᔐ

READER

I hope that your life together encompasses the wonder of nature—that
it reflects elements of simplicity, exuberance, beauty, silence, color,
and a concordance with the rhythms of life and love.

ᔐᔐᔐᔐᔐᔐ

READER

We wish for you a home—not merely a place of stone and wood, but
an island of sanity and serenity in a frenzied world, where your love
will always abide. We wish for you the blessings of good health and
good fortune.

ᔐᔐᔐᔐᔐᔐ

READER

It is the dawn of a new day, and we are here to witness the dawning
of a new life for Donna and Alan.

Just as the river finds its way to the ocean, and the rain finds its way
to the earth, so should this man and woman find each other.

As the tree finds its way to the sky, and the bird finds its way to the nest,
so should this man and woman find their way into each other's arms.

Along with the night, there is the day; the ocean and the sky merge in
the distance to form the horizon. The past and the future fuse themselves together to form the moment in which we live.

There is a reality known as love, and as witnessed by us it does contain beauty. It is our future. Nurture it, care for it, and call it your child.

✣✣✣✣✣

READER

Above you are the stars; below you is the earth. As time passes, remember: Let your love be as constant as the stars. Let your love be as firm as the earth. Be close, yet allow each other to breathe. Possess one another, yet encourage each other to soar free. Have patience with each other, and understanding, for this will enable the storms that will come to pass through more quickly. Be free in the giving of affection and warmth. Make love often, and be sensuous with one another. Have no fear, and do not allow the ways and words of the unenlightened to give you unease. For the Goddess and the God are with you, now and always.

✣✣✣✣✣

The Seven Hebrew Wedding Blessings

Blessed art Thou, O Lord our God, King of the universe, who created the fruit of the vine, symbol of joy.

Blessed art Thou, O Lord our God, King of the universe, who has created all things to Thy glory.

Blessed art Thou, O Lord our God, King of the universe, Creator of man.

Blessed art Thou, O Lord our God, King of the universe, who has made man in Thine image after Thy likeness, and has fashioned woman from man as his mate, that together they may perpetuate life. Blessed art Thou, O Lord, Creator of man.

May Zion rejoice as her children are restored to her in joy. Blessed art Thou, O Lord, who causes Zion to rejoice at her children's return.

O make these loved companions greatly to rejoice, even as of old Thou didst gladden Thy creatures in the Garden of Eden. Blessed art Thou, O Lord, who makest bridegroom and bride to rejoice.

Blessed art Thou, O Lord our God, King of the universe, who has created joy and gladness, bridegroom and bride, mirth and exultation, pleasure and delight, love, brotherhood, peace and fellowship. Soon may there be heard in the cities of Judah, and in the streets of Jerusalem, the voice of joy and gladness, the voice of the bridegroom and the voice of the bride, the jubilant voices of those joined in marriage under the bridal canopy, and of youths feasting and singing. Blessed art Thou, O Lord, who makest the bridegroom to rejoice with the bride.

Amen.[8]

꒰꒰꒰꒰꒰

Eight Contemporary Blessings

A different person presents each of the following blessings, wishes, offerings or gifts. For example, each member of the wedding party can read one.

FIRST GIFT GIVER

We bless this couple in the name of Friendship.

(or—We offer this couple the gift of Friendship.)

May this marriage prosper in the passing years with the strengthening bonds of two who know, trust, and savor each other.

SECOND GIFT GIVER

We bless this couple in the name of Intimacy.

May this marriage discover the satisfaction of deep sharing.

THIRD GIFT GIVER

We bless this couple in the name of Justice.

May this marriage seek what is fine and right and flourish with love and respect.

FOURTH GIFT GIVER

We bless this couple in the name of Wisdom.

May this marriage write a new chapter in the book of experience, husband and wife each learning from the other.

FIFTH GIFT GIVER

We bless this couple in the name of Joy.

May this marriage hear the song of gladness, through word of mouth and meditation of heart.

SIXTH GIFT GIVER

We bless this couple in the name of Creativity.

May this marriage create special dreams, and revel in their fulfillment.

SEVENTH GIFT GIVER

We bless this couple in the name of Appreciation.

May this marriage flourish, as they keep their hearts open to each other, day and night.

EIGHTH GIFT GIVER

We bless this couple in the name of Kindness.

May this marriage show that these two can treat each other always with generosity and good will.

CELEBRANT

We bless this wine, a gift of the earth, the sun, and the rain.

May the sharing of this cup symbolize the sharing of your life together, giving to each other and receiving from each other, with enthusiasm and delight.

જ્ઞજ્ઞજ્ઞજ્ઞજ્ઞ

Love is a canvas furnished by Nature
and embroidered by imagination

— Voltaire

Chapter 13

Putting It All Together

I wonder by my troth,
what thou and I did till we lov'd?

—John Donne

You've finished creating or selecting the major parts of your wedding ceremony. Now put it all together so that it flows smoothly. It is easier to organize the various parts if you separate each section, then shuffle and reshuffle the pieces until you get the sequence you want.

We don't have to tell you that the beginning comes first and the closing comes last. Usually the celebrant's address and the couple's statements of appreciation come soon after the opening, but place them in the order that seems most natural to you.

The vows, ring exchange, and kiss are the climax of the ceremony and usually come just before the closing.

Look carefully at each of the remaining components to decide where you want them. Sometimes there's an obvious logic to where a particular piece belongs. For example, if the parents are going to welcome each of you as new members of their families, you may want to place that exchange near the beginning. If a child is being acknowledged, it makes sense to put that part after the couple's statements of appreciation to each other.

There's plenty of room for creativity here, and no absolute rights or wrongs. Just ask yourselves if there's a natural place for a component to go.

Poetry, readings, music, and rituals add variety and pacing. Place them throughout the ceremony, as transitions, or to separate the various parts. Use a group of readings as a section by itself, perhaps after the celebrant's address or the statements of appreciation.

A wine ritual typically comes just before or after the vows. It is a visual expression of the couple's commitment to share their lives with each other, just as the vows are the verbal expression, and the rings are the tangible symbol of that commitment.

Arrange the different parts, read through the whole ceremony and decide whether you are both happy with the order. You may need to add a line or two to make graceful transitions from one component to another, or to introduce or explain a ritual or a reading. If anything still seems rough, reshuffle and rewrite. If there are trouble spots that still don't work, mark them and go on. Once everything is in order, put the whole ceremony aside and come back to it in a day or two. Do you like the way you have organized everything, or are you uncomfortable with some areas? If you reach a roadblock or want a third party's perspective, ask for advice from your celebrant or a friend with writing skills.

ॐॐॐॐॐ

No partner in a love relationship
...should feel that he has to give up
an essential part of himself to make it viable.
—May Sarton

Chapter 14

Rehearsing and Preparing

Give her two red roses, each with a note.
The first note says, "For the woman I love"
and the second, "For my best friend."
— Anonymous

Here we are at the next to the last step. The hard work is over. This is the fun part. In this chapter we will walk you through your rehearsal and give you some suggestions for preparing yourselves for the ceremony itself.

༄ ༄ ༄

Planning the Rehearsal

We recommend that you *do* have a rehearsal. Not a dress rehearsal, which is equivalent to a full performance, but a chance to work out all the kinks so that the ceremony will flow smoothly. Sometimes couples feel that there is nothing to rehearse—that it's not worth the time. This *may* be true of a small, simple wedding, but usually a rehearsal is worthwhile. Not only will everyone in the wedding party be sure of exactly where they are to stand and how they are to get there, but you can work out the logistics of rings and bouquets, wine bottles and wine glasses, poetry and music, and make it clear to everyone.

Hold the rehearsal at the site where you will have the ceremony. If possible, do it shortly before the wedding: the day before is best, but some people prefer to make it earlier in the week. If it is impossible to hold the rehearsal on site, do it someplace else and improvise.

Everyone who has a part in the ceremony should be present at the rehearsal. Be sure that anyone who is not present is thoroughly coached. It is also important to have all the props on hand for the rehearsal: rings, mock bouquet, wine, glasses, tape recorder, music, and so on.

By the time you get to the rehearsal, your ceremony should be in its final form. You will then know the sequence of each element of the ceremony. Sometimes, however, you will find that the things you had planned don't go smoothly: the kiss followed by the wine ceremony doesn't seem to flow; it feels awkward to stand still during the long musical piece; the formation you thought would work isn't right for the site you've chosen. The purpose of the rehearsal is to detect such problems and solve them. During the rehearsal, you will also figure out myriad details. How will the bride handle her bouquet, his ring, and her vows all at once? Where will the wine and glasses be? Who will reach for them? Who will open the bottle and when? What will you do with the glasses during the kiss?

꒰ꞋꞋ꒱ ꒰ꞋꞋ꒱ ꒰ꞋꞋ꒱

Staging the Ceremony

A key consideration is the staging of the ceremony. Where will each member of the wedding party stand? In a church wedding, the bride and groom traditionally stand facing the celebrant with their backs to their guests. Often the celebrant is on a dais above the couple, which makes him or her the center of attention. This is not consistent with the modern approach that focuses attention on the marrying couple.

In contemporary ceremonies, the bride and groom are given the positions of honor. Typically, they form the center of a semicircle made up of all the members of the wedding party and they stand facing their guests. If a wedding is a small one, they may stand within the circle of their guests. The accompanying diagrams suggest several possibilities. Whether you want your guests to stand or sit during the ceremony will also influence the formation that you choose.

❧ ❧ ❧

SUGGESTED FORMATIONS FOR CONTEMPORARY WEDDING CEREMONIES

Traditional Formation:

Rarely used in contemporary ceremonies. Bride and groom face celebrant; guests are seated.

Typical Formation for a Contemporary Ceremony:

Wedding party faces guests in a semicircle. Bride and groom stand side by side. Guests are standing or sitting.

Alternative Formation for a Contemporary Ceremony:

Wedding party faces the guests and the celebrant faces the wedding party and the guests. Guests are standing or sitting.

Formal Formation:

Wedding party faces the seated guests. The celebrant stands between the bride and groom. The bride and groom turn slightly to face each other.

Alternative Formation for a Formal or Informal Ceremony:

Bride and groom face each other while standing in front of the celebrant. The celebrant faces the guests. The guests are standing or sitting.

Circle Formation for a Small Ceremony:

Wedding party and guests all stand in a circle.

✧✧✧✧✧

Once you have decided on the formation, you must determine how to get everyone into position. Do you want a processional in which everyone in the wedding party walks down the aisle? Do you want to gather informally when the wedding is about to begin and simply tell everyone to take their places? Do you want the celebrant, bridesmaids, and ushers to be in place while the bride (and perhaps the groom) walks down the aisle? You may have any variation on these arrangements. Your decision will depend partly on your own feelings and partly on the facility where the wedding is held. Some environments simply do not lend themselves to a processional, while others seem to demand it. Remember, a processional does not require a long, straight aisle. You can wander through the trees, along a meadow path, come into the garden from the house, or parade down the stairway.

If your facility has a middle aisle, you will have to decide whether you want to divide the bride's family and friends from the groom's or allow everyone to sit where they please.

Pay attention to the symbolism of the processional. It may be appropriate for the father of a young bride to escort his daughter down the aisle. Such an arrangement may not be appropriate for a couple already living together, an older couple, or a couple who have been previously married.

✌ ✌ ✌

The Final Run-Through

Let's take the rehearsal from the beginning. First, make sure everyone knows exactly where to stand, how to get to that spot, and in what order. Now walk everybody through to this point. It is helpful to have an observer placed where your guests will be, to offer suggestions and comment on how things look and sound.

Pay attention to the way people walk, how they stand, where they direct their attention, and how quickly or slowly they move. Notice how each person reaches his or her place—does anyone have to cross in front of anyone else or make any awkward turns? How does it look when you are all in place? Should you be closer together? Make whatever adjustments are necessary and walk through it again.

Next, read through the ceremony. Make sure everyone knows their cues. Listen carefully. Are the transitions smooth? Where is the emphasis? Are people reading loudly enough? Are they reading slowly and clearly? Voices are usually hard to hear outdoors. It is especially important that the bride and groom practice saying their parts loudly, because our natural tendency in moments of strong emotion and tension is to lower our voices to a whisper or to speak too rapidly.

ॐ ॐ ॐ

To Read or To Memorize—
and Other Considerations

Don't try to memorize your lines! It is perfectly acceptable to read from cards or from an attractive folder that you have prepared for the ceremony. Unless you have had acting experience, it is not likely that you will memorize your lines well enough to speak easily. It is far better to know your part very well *and* to have cue cards handy for reference. You may prefer to repeat the words after the celebrant, but if you do, take care not to trivialize your vows: make sure each brief phrase retains its meaning and significance.

As you rehearse the ceremony, pay particular attention to those places that require planning and coordination. A typical trouble spot is in the exchange of rings. The bride has a bouquet in one hand, a cue card in the other, and her maid of honor is holding the ring for the groom. How does the bride get the ring and hand over the bouquet? It's all very simple if you plan in advance, and very awkward if you don't.

Any other rituals or parts that require props are potential trouble spots. Pay careful attention to them and work out the logistics.

If, as part of your ceremony, you want your guests to speak spontaneously, it is important to "salt the audience" by asking two or three friends, in advance, to prepare to say something. This will increase the likelihood that others will feel free to express themselves.

The closing requires particularly careful rehearsal. When you have read the closing statement, how will you let people know that the ceremony is over? How will you make the transition from ceremony to congratulations? A recessional is an easy way of

making this transition, but it is not often used in informal ceremonies. It is sometimes appropriate to have the attendants or
parents break ranks and go to congratulate the newly married
couple. Or the couple can go directly to their parents or new in-laws
for hugs and kisses. It helps to cue in a few people in advance,
telling them what you want, so that others in the audience can
follow their lead. People have a tendency to stay put at such times
if they are not sure what you expect them to do. An appropriate
musical accompaniment can make the transition even smoother and
more definite.

ॐ ॐ ॐ

Details, Details, Details

Now let's take a look at some details about the ceremony
itself. What time is it scheduled to start? Is that the time you
actually plan to start? Who must be present before you begin the
ceremony? What if Grandma is late?

How will you let your guests know that the ceremony is about
to begin? Will your ushers guide them to their places?

How will the wedding party know when the guests are in
place? Who will cue the musicians when it is time to begin? It is
important that the celebrant, the wedding coordinator, or a friend
take charge of coordinating these aspects of the ceremony.

Okay. Now you've done the entire rehearsal. You've worked
out all the rough spots. Stop and think for a minute. Is there
anything else that can go wrong? You could forget you cue cards,
leave your rings or license at home, the flowers might not arrive, or
the caterer might have a flat tire. Anything can go wrong and there
is no way to guard against all mishaps. You have done everything
possible. Even if something terrible happens—like forgetting the
rings—your ceremony can still be beautiful. It all depends on your
attitude. Borrow a ring from someone else if you have to. Look
over the celebrant's shoulder if you've forgotten your own cue
card. Just let it go if the ring rolls off into the grass. Today's catas-
trophe will make you smile tomorrow. Flow with the events and all

will work out just fine. If you can laugh and relax, the focus will be where it should be—on the meaning of the ceremony—and flaws will seem less important.

༄ ༄ ༄

Preparing Yourselves: Just Before the Ceremony

You have a choice. You can either be apprehensive, worried about all the last minute details, rushed, confused, tense, anxious— or you can be relaxed, savoring every precious moment of this rich experience, leaving yourself open to delight, joy, and happiness.

How you prepare for The Day and how you choose to experience it is entirely up to you. Here are some hints that may make your wedding day easier and more like the day you want it to be.

DECIDE NOT TO LET ANYTHING HASSLE YOU

Sure there's too much to do. You may never have done this before, but there are many people who want to help you. Delegate! Make this a day when you start sentences with "Would you please do me a favor...?" Don't take on the anxiety of others—parents, your soon-to-be-spouse, jittery friends, anyone. Decide that you will be an island of serenity in the sea of chaos.

INDULGE YOURSELF!

If you like to sleep late, have everything out of the way the night before so that you start the day in the best possible mood. Give yourself enough time for a long bath or shower, time to dress carefully, a chance to go for a quiet walk or eat a leisurely meal. Pamper yourself in the ways that you know best—get your hair just so or get an extra special shave, take time with the kids, have a telephone visit with your best friend, or just take time to be by yourself. Don't wait until the last minute to leave for the wedding: you have enough on your mind today and you don't need a speeding ticket. Be good to yourself.

QUIET TIME

You've selected someone you trust to oversee the details. Now give yourself the seclusion you deserve, before the ceremony. Choose whether you will spend this quiet time together or alone, and then find a quiet, private place where you can contemplate what you are about to do.

EXPECT THE UNEXPECTED

Every effective planner plans for the unanticipated: the humorous remark of a small child during a serious moment in the ceremony; a misplaced ring; a lost best man; a late wedding cake. These can try your patience and ingenuity. Face each unexpected occurrence with ease and good humor. Your guests are not critics. They bring tons of goodwill. They're with you to share your joy. Your mood will set the mood for those around you.

LET THE WEDDING UNFOLD!

You've done the hard part. You've checked the checklists and delegated tasks to others; you've covered all the bases. From now on the wedding takes on a life of its own. There's a beginning, middle, and end. Let it happen. It's going to be great!

వావావావావా

Marriage resembles a pair of shears,
so joined that they cannot be separated;
often moving in opposite directions;
yet always punishing anyone
who comes between them.

—Sydney Smith

Chapter 15

A Collection of
Contemporary Ceremonies

*We love because it is
the only true adventure.*

—Nikki Giovanni

This chapter offers an array of ceremonies. Some are philosophical, others lighthearted; some are symbolic or poetic, others more down to earth. In some ceremonies the celebrant takes a primary role. Others include parent and guest participation. Some contain many rituals and others are minimal and just meet legal requirements.

Let these examples stimulate your imagination and help you develop the tone *you* want.

ॐ ॐ ॐ

Typical Contemporary Ceremonies

RITUALS, SYMBOLS, AND DISTINCTIVE VOWS

This ceremony includes traditional wedding elements along with romantic poems as appreciations, and highly personal vows.

ꕔꕔꕔꕔꕔ

Opening

The celebrant, groom and best woman are in place. A trio plays Handel's "Water Music." The bridesmaids and groomsmen enter in pairs, followed by the matron of honor. The music changes, the guests are asked to stand, and the bride enters accompanied by her father. They walk down the aisle, the groom comes forward to meet his bride, and they stand slightly to one side of the celebrant facing the guests.

CELEBRANT

Thank you for being with us today. You are the people who have helped Kelly and Krista to become who they are. You are the people who mean the most to them, who have shared their lives, who have provided for them, who have nourished them and inspired them.

You are the ones who have believed in them and encouraged them, and now you are here to share this life-changing moment with them. Some people who are important to Krista and Kelly are not here with us today, and we want to acknowledge them also: especially Krista's grandmother, Toni, who is treasured in memory. She is here in spirit, and in our hearts.

Now, let us join together to celebrate the love of Krista and Kelly. They have found with each other such deep companionship, and a love so strong and vital, that they wish publicly to join their lives in marriage.

They have learned that falling in love with another person is like the exploration of a wild and lovely place; and that loving one another has deepened their connection to all of life. They have found that the intimacy and the surprises of that experience are a form of reverence and wholeness. And it is this feeling of joy and wonder that they want to share with you on this, their wedding day.

A wedding ceremony is an outward declaration of something that is inner and real: a sacred, personal union that nature might mirror, a church solemnize, or a state declare legal, but which only love can create.

Let us take a moment to be silent together, to remember why we are here, the meaning this event has for each of us, and what each of us wishes for this beautiful couple. (*A moment of silence.*)

Celebrant's best wishes for the couple

May Kelly and Krista discover joy, excitement, and a sense of possibility and challenge in the high work they are about to undertake.

May they find peace of heart and strength of spirit so that they may honor the vows they make here today. And may the promises they make inspire and instruct each one of us who celebrates with them.

The search for our life's partner is a yearning for completion, a yearning to share what is most essential in our natures: life and its essence, love.

Welcome by the family combined with a flower ritual

CELEBRANT

The joining of Krista and Kelly is also the joining of their families, integrating their different traditions, strengthening the family tree.

Terry and Lindsay, as Krista's parents, do you offer this couple your goodwill? Do you welcome Kelly as a member of your family and grant him your love and affection?

BRIDE'S PARENTS

We do. (*Kelly gives flowers to Krista's parents.*)

CELEBRANT

Don and Joan, as Kelly's parents, do you offer this couple your goodwill? Do you welcome Krista as a member of your family and grant her your love and affection?

GROOM'S PARENTS

We do. (*Krista gives flowers to Kelly's parents.*)

Reading

CELEBRANT

Leslie has offered to enrich today's celebration with a reading from Rainer Marie Rilke.

FRIEND (from *Letters*, Rainer Maria Rilke)

Marriage is in many ways a simplification of life, and it naturally combines the strengths and wills of two young people so that, together, they seem to reach farther into the future than they did before. Above all, marriage is a new task and a new seriousness, a new demand on the strength and generosity of each partner, and a great danger to both.

The point of marriage is not to create a quick commonality by tearing down all boundaries; on the contrary, a good marriage is one in which each partner appoints the other to be the guardian of his solitude, and thus they show each other the greatest possible trust. A merging of two people is an impossibility, and where it seems to exist, it is a hemming-in, a mutual consent that robs one party or both parties of their fullest freedom and development. But once the realization is accepted that even between the closest people infinite distances exist, a marvelous living side-by-side can grow up for them, if they succeed in loving the expanse between them, which gives them the possibility of always seeing each other as a whole and before an immense sky....

To take love seriously and to undergo it and learn it like a profession—that is what young people need to do. Like so many other things, people have also misunderstood the position love has in life; they have made it into play and pleasure because they thought that play and pleasure are more blissful than work; but there is nothing happier than work, and love, precisely because it is the supreme happiness, can be nothing other than work—so those who love must try to act as if they had a great work to accomplish: they must be much alone and go into themselves and gather and concentrate themselves; they must work; they must become something.

For the more we are, the richer everything we experience is. And those who want to have a deep love in their lives must collect and save for it, and gather honey.

Celebrant's address

CELEBRANT

Kelly and Krista, your marriage actually began the moment the two of you first decided to join your lives together. Today, we merely acknowledge the bond that continues to grow between you, as you take this next important step. No words that I say can create your marriage; only the two of you can do that.

Your marriage is unique: there has never been another like it, nor will there be one like it ever again. For of the billions of people who inhabit our planet, you have found and chosen each other! The possibilities before you are limitless. You will never finish building this relationship, and together you will find new ways to nourish each other's lives, while finding greater happiness and meaning in your own.

Your relationship abounds with goodwill. Although you have each been brought up in different households, with different traditions and experiences, you have found much you value in common. And now we ask you, different as you are, to grow for the rest of your lives—both as individuals and as a couple—and to continue to cherish each other.

Promise never to take each other for granted. Remind yourselves often of what has drawn you together. Take the time to make your partner feel special. Take the time to play together. Take the time to listen, and to share, and to negotiate; to talk about fears and failures and disappointments; to talk about each other's expectations, hopes, and dreams.

Above all, take the time to tell each other what you want, take the risk of being vulnerable with each other. A good marriage takes time and effort, courage and commitment.

Sometimes, communication can be difficult; give each other the benefit of the doubt. Learn to listen to the music, not just the words.

You have our best wishes, our hopes, our high expectations, and our love as you undertake this rewarding journey!

Three-glass wine ritual

Music as background to the wine ritual: Fauré's "Pavanne."

CELEBRANT
Wine is a gift from the earth, the rain and the sun. From the most ancient of times drinking from the same cup has been a powerful

symbol of affection, of agreement, and of peace. Sipping from the same cup is symbolic of the life the couple will share, each giving to the other generously, each receiving from the other freely and fully.

In a variation of the time-honored wedding tradition of sharing wine, Kelly and Krista will each sip first from their own glass, indicating that they will maintain their independence and individuality. (*They toast each other and sip.*)

Then, to symbolize the strong bond that exists between them, they will exchange glasses, and drink from each other's cup. (*The couple exchange glasses, toast and sip.*)

Finally, to symbolize the creation of this marriage, Kelly and Krista will each pour some of their own wine into a third cup and hold that for each other as they drink. (*Kelly and Krista each pour their wine into a common glass, then each holds the glass as the other sips.*)

Couple's statements of appreciation using poetry

GROOM (untitled, Rumi)
> *This love is as good as oil and honey to the throat,*
> *as linen to the body,*
> *as fine garments to the gods,*
> *as incense to worshippers when they enter in,*
> *as the little seal ring to my finger.*
>
> *It is like a ripe pear in a man's hand,*
> *it is like the dates we mix with wine,*
> *it is like the seeds the baker adds to bread.*
>
> *We will be together even when old age comes.*
>
> *And the days in between will be food set before us,*
> *dates and honey, bread and wine.*[9]

BRIDE (from *Persian Love Poem*, Rumi)
> *The time span of union is eternity.*
> *This life is a jar, and in it, union is the pure wine.*
> *If we aren't together, of what use is the jar?*

The moment I heard my first love story I began seeking you,
not realizing the search was useless.
Lovers don't meet somewhere along the way.
They're in one another's souls from the beginning.

You are the sea, I am a fish....

I am a crystal goblet in my Love's hand.
Look into my eyes if you don't believe me.

Vows

CELEBRANT *(to guests)*

Now, as Krista and Kelly prepare to exchange their vows, I ask all of you present to use this moment to remember your *own* promises, and to re-commit yourselves to the pledges you have made.

GROOM

Krista, I wrote my vows to reflect my love for you, and your love for baseball.

I'll be there for rain delays
called strike threes
and the occasional swing-and-a-miss.

I'll be there for the walk,
the balk, and the pitchout.

I'll be there for the steal.
I'll be there for the pop-fly,
the ground out, the earned run in.

I'll be there from the first to the ninth,
and extra innings galore.

But no matter the course of the game,
it's the outcome that matters.
You are the perfect game,
the stolen base,
the grandslam,
the inside-the-park home run.

You are my wife, my love, my future.

BRIDE

Kelly, I promise you my love, understanding, and encouragement. I will support you if you are fearful, I will inspire you if you are doubtful, I will comfort you if you are sad. I will love and trust you unconditionally.

Individually, we are words, colors, and seasons; together, we are a poem, a painting, a year.

The rings

CELEBRANT

Words are powerful, but fleeting, and the sound of them is soon gone. Therefore, the wedding ring becomes the enduring symbol of the promises we have just heard.

(*To the Best Woman*) Sandy, may I have the rings please?

Rings are an ancient symbol, blessed and simple. Round like the sun, like a perfect pearl, like arms that embrace—circles, for love that is given comes back round again and again.

May these symbols remind you that your love, like the sun, illuminates; that your love, like the pearl, grows in luster; and that your love, like arms that embrace, is a grace upon this world.

These are very special rings—handed down through the generations from grandparents and great-grandparents, binding this couple—not only to each other—but to their families.

Now let us witness the sealing of your promises with these rings.

GROOM

Krista, I give you this ring, an endless circle with no beginning and no end, as a symbol of my love. With this ring, I thee wed. (*Places ring on her finger.*)

BRIDE

Kelly, I give you this ring, an endless circle with no beginning and no end, as a symbol of my love. With this ring, I thee wed. (*Places ring on his finger.*)

Celebrant's blessings

CELEBRANT

> May the steps you have just taken toward each other help you to grow in awareness of yourselves, as well as in your love and understanding of each other.

> We wish for you a home that is a haven from the turmoil of the world, a place of harmony and peace, security and strength. Trusting each other, may you trust life, and never be afraid.

> And may the affection and joy you share radiate, enriching the lives of your families, your friends, and all whose lives you touch.

> *(To the guests)* We know not what the future may bring into the life of this couple, but we pray that together they may be equal to the needs of their tomorrows. May they find in all times an ever-growing love.

> Krista and Kelly seek the blessings of those who are gathered here. They treasure your wisdom, and ask for your support.

Responsive reading

CELEBRANT

> I ask you all to join me in a responsive reading of an Apache Wedding Prayer to demonstrate to Krista and Kelly our support of their commitment:

> *Now you will feel no rain,*

GUESTS

> *for each of you will be a shelter to the other;*

CELEBRANT

> *Now you will feel no cold,*

GUESTS

> *for each of you will be warmth to the other;*

CELEBRANT

> *Now there is no more loneliness,*

GUESTS

> *for each of you will be companion to the other;*

CELEBRANT
Now you are two bodies,
GUESTS
but there is only one life before you.
CELEBRANT
Go now to your dwelling place
and enter into the days of your togetherness
GUESTS
and may your days be good and long upon the earth.

The breaking of the wine glass

CELEBRANT

To conclude our ceremony, we observe an ancient custom, the breaking of the wine glass. The shattering of this glass symbolizes that what matters most in life is the spirit, not the letter; the wine, not the cup. It also symbolizes that our joy in this union is so great that no vessel can contain it.

As Kelly now breaks this glass, let us all join in and rejoice with them with the sound of celebration. (*The groom crushes the wrapped glass with his heel.*)

Closing: pronouncement, final blessings, kiss, and recessional

CELEBRANT

Kelly and Krista, in expressing your private affirmations you have pronounced yourselves husband and wife. You have vowed to be loyal and loving toward each other, formalizing in our presence the existence of the bond already between you.

(*To the guests*) I call on all of you to witness that Krista and Kelly have exchanged their vows, and according the laws of the State of New York, they are now husband and wife.

(*To the couple*) May all blessings attend you, may joy pervade your lives together, may your home be forever a place of peace and true fulfillment.

From this moment on, venture your separate ways together, remembering always to be each other's best and truest friend.

Krista, you may now kiss the groom! (*They kiss.*)

The recessional music starts. The couple leads the wedding party out.

৵ৎ ৵ৎ ৵ৎ

A SHORT SYMBOLIC CEREMONY: THE MEANING OF THE RINGS

This couple's rings were made by a friend who presented them during the ceremony. The symbols on the rings were carefully chosen to represent the cycles of life, a symbolism that was also incorporated in the ceremony.

৵ৎ৵ৎ৵ৎ৵ৎ৵ৎ

Opening and celebrant's address

A friend plays a guitar softly. The wedding party gathers under an arch of flowers near the edge of a cliff. They stand, waiting for the guests to turn their attention to the ceremony.

CELEBRANT

Dear friends, we have gathered here on this cliff overlooking the Pacific Ocean to celebrate the marriage of David and Judith. Oceans both connect and separate us, just as connections and separations flow through a marriage. Like marriages, oceans can be calm and peaceful, or turbulent and stormy. While we skim across the surface of the sea, we are aware of the immense and unknown depths that lie below us. We are aware that as we skim through the everyday activities of marriage, we are upheld by the profound, mysterious and unplumbed world beneath us. Standing on this high bluff we experience the power of this geographical metaphor for marriage: its heights of joy, its depths of discomfort — and the ever-constant, ever-changing beauty and wonder of a boundless commitment of two people to each other.

Affection, respect, and commitment form the bedrock of a marriage: they provide the support and sustenance that allow tenderness, love, and intimacy to flourish. To love devotedly means to grow in consciousness.

Love breathes more deeply as we grow in awareness. At the core of such awareness in marriage are care and concern, giving and sharing, a strength and intimacy that leaves no room for fear or distrust. To love devotedly requires honesty, the kind of honesty where being true to oneself means being true to the other. The goal is total communication. Judith and David have found in each other someone with whom to be honest, with whom to be at ease, with whom to be at home.

Judith and David, I invite you to exchange your vows.

Vows

GROOM

Judith, I accept you as my wife and my friend, to love devotedly, to honor faithfully, to reach for completely, to grow with through all the days to come.

BRIDE

David, I accept you as my husband and my friend, to love devotedly, to honor faithfully, to reach for completely, to grow with through all the days to come.

Ring ceremony

CELEBRANT

Will the Maker of the Rings please step forward? (*The Ring Maker presents the rings to the bride and groom.*)

BRIDE

This ring, with the Sun and Moon upon it, is a symbol of my constant love for you through all the cycles of time.

GROOM

This ring, with the Sun and Moon upon it, is a symbol of my constant love for you through all the cycles of time.

Pronouncement

CELEBRANT

In the presence of all here assembled, and by the power invested in me by the State of California, I now pronounce you husband and wife.

Music. The couple goes to their guests to receive hugs and best wishes.

ॐ ॐ ॐ

Poetic Ceremonies

A RESPONSIVE READING: *OF THE FIRST KISS*

In this ceremony the couple creatively fashions a favorite passage into a shared reading. They felt free to make minor changes. We give the quotation in its original form.

৵৵৵৵৵

Opening

GROOM

Barbara and I welcome you, our family and friends, to a celebration of our love and our union.

Statements of appreciation

BRIDE

We want to share our wedding with you. We want you to feel a part of our celebration. For that reason, we have given each of you a rose. We have chosen this flower as a symbol of our love, which began with our first kiss.

Of the First Kiss, **Kahlil Gibran**

BRIDE *and* GROOM (*alternate reading each sentence of the following:*)

It is the first sip from the cup filled by the goddess with the nectar of Life. It is the dividing line between Doubt that beguiles the spirit and saddens the heart, and Certitude that floods the inner self with joy.

It is the beginning of the song of Life and the first act in the drama of the Ideal Man. It is the bond that unites the strangeness of the past with the brightness of the future; the link between the silence of the feelings and their song. It is a word uttered by four lips proclaiming the heart a throne, Love a king, and fidelity a crown. It is the gentle touch of the delicate fingers of the breeze on the lips of the rose— uttering a long sigh of relief and a sweet moan.

It is the beginning of that magic vibration that carries lovers from the world of weights and measures into the world of dreams and revelations.

It is the union of two fragrant flowers; and the mingling of their fragrance toward the creation of a third soul.

As the first glance is like a seed sown by the goddess in the field of the human heart, so the first kiss is the first flower at the tip of the branch of the Tree of Life.

BRIDE *and* GROOM *(in unison)*

So our union in marriage is the first fruit of the first flowering kiss which grew from that first glance.

Reading

FRIEND (from A.C. Benson)

A young husband and wife came to stay with us in all the first flush of married happiness. One realized all day long that other people merely made a pleasant background for their love, and that for each there was but one real figure on the scene. This was borne witness to by a whole armory of gentle looks, swift glances, silent gestures. They were both full to the brim of a delicate laughter, of over-brimming wonder, of tranquil desire. And we all took a part in their gracious happiness.

. . . So the sweet hour passed and left a fragrance behind it; whatever might befall, they had tasted of the holy wine of joy, they had blessed the cup, and bidden us, too, to set our lips to it.[10]

Vows and rings

GROOM

This I vow, Barbara: to love you. To hold you dear, yet not too close, to take pride in your successes and not fear your growth; to listen to your heart, yet not try to read your mind. And always to love you for your dignity, your spirit, your beauty, and your gentleness of heart.

Barbara my love, be my companion and my wife. Accept my ring and let us begin our marriage.

BRIDE

I accept your ring, which now encircles my heart's finger, as your love encircles me. I celebrate my love and joy of us. I accept you unconditionally as my friend, companion, lover, and husband. And I vow enduring affection, loyalty, trust, candor, and love.

John, my love, be my husband. Accept my ring, and let us begin our marriage.

GROOM

I accept your ring and your love, and I welcome you as my wife.

Wine Ritual and Kiss

Best man pours wine; bride and groom drink, arms entwined, then hand their glasses to their attendants, and kiss.

Pronouncement and closing

CELEBRANT

John and Barbara have made their vows and exchanged rings. They are now husband and wife. Let our celebration begin!

Music, applause, balloons!

ॐ ॐ ॐ

A LIGHTHEARTED CEREMONY

This wedding took place in the late spring in a flower-strewn meadow. It is a poetic and playful reflection of the couple's long-standing relationship.

ঞ'ঞ'ঞ'ঞ'ঞ

Opening

CELEBRANT

Harold and Meg have been together for eight years now. Today they have asked us to come together in celebration of their love and to take part in this ceremony: a public dedication to the continuation of their lives as one.

Statements of Appreciation

BRIDE

You are my best friend: we play, laugh, and cry together; we philosophize and solve the world's problems.

You are my punching bag: I tickle and wrestle my frustrations out on you.

You are my silly child with scratched nose and fumbly feet. I laugh with you, my heart bursting with joy.

You are my strength when I'm weak and afraid of the world and myself, you make me feel whole and good again.

You are my lover we share our minds, bodies, and souls completely.

In being all this you are my husband.

GROOM

It's hard to put into words what we communicate every day: love, trust, respect. There are plenty of good words, but they're all completely empty without someone to discover them with. Together we've lived these words, sharing and growing in a way that seems as honest and true as this land around us today: feeling happiness and sorrow, tension and peace, each in our own way and time. But encircling it all is the oneness we feel, the house sheltering our separate lives, bringing us together at the end of every day.

Readings by the bride and groom

BRIDE (*The Wife*, Denise Levertov)

A frog under you
knees drawn up
ready to leap out of time

A dog beside you
snuffing at you, seeking
scent of you, an idea unformulated

I give up on trying to answer my question
Do I love you enough?
It's enough to be
so much here. And
Certainly when I catch
your mind in the
act of plucking
truthfromthedarksurroundingnowhere
As a swallow skims a gnat from the
        deep sky
I don't stop to ask myself
Do I love him? but
        laugh for joy.

GROOM

The sun comes up
A morning breeze dances outside
        the window.
At my side you are still dreaming,
A warm, fuzzy animal
My thoughts turn through the day to
come, and fall through those now past.
Beyond our tiny house many fields lie
in waste, caked with dust and sorrow.
I walk out into our garden, thinking
        of you, and smile.

Readings by friends

FRIEND *(The Greatest Gift* [adapted], Katharine Whiteside Taylor)
All things I would give my love,
All things tender, caring, serving, true.
I would enwrap him in my loving arms
And shield him from all stress and pain.
I would enchant him with the vision bright
Of those rare gifts that are his deepest self.
And I would carry him on wings of joy
To all the heights the soul of man can know.

And yet, I wonder if perhaps
Love's greatest gift I have forgot—
The final gift
More costing and more painful than all else
The gift of freedom
To be just himself
To stand alone
Apart from me
And choose his own true way
wherever it may lead.

Vows and rings

BRIDE

Harold, I take you as my husband and I am happy to be your wife. This ring is a symbol of all we have shared and of our continuing happiness together.

GROOM

Meg, I give myself as your husband and take you as my wife. This ring is a symbol of all we have shared and of our continuing happiness together.

Closing: Pronouncement and kiss

CELEBRANT

Meg and Harold, you have married each other. May your lives be filled with delight. Meg, you may kiss the groom!

Kiss, laughter, applause

ॐ ॐ ॐ

Ceremonies for Special Situations

Noteworthy circumstances, such as second marriages, weddings of older couples, or nuptials taking place on holidays, allow the couple to create a distinctive ceremony.

FINDING LOVE AGAIN

In this ceremony, the couple uses metaphor and poetic images to express their joy in having found each other.

ॐॐॐॐॐ

Music and Processional
Opening

CELEBRANT

True love finds its culmination in a lifelong commitment, and a wedding ceremony joyously celebrates that commitment, in the presence of family and friends.

Today Bob and Cathy enter the next phase of their growing relationship by publicly declaring their love for each other and their intention to live together for the rest of their lives. Cathy and Bob embody a love that aims to share the future with each other, and we are privileged and delighted to be present as they embark on that sacred journey.

Statements of appreciation

BRIDE

Bob, my love, time has brought us together. Time has given us life. There are birds now, and stars, the oceans, and flowers, and beautiful sunrises and sunsets. There is you and me, playing, loving, talking, understanding, daring, giving, and living.

I am alive with you, my love.
I never wanted to touch a man the way I want to touch you.

I never wanted to love a man the way I want to love you.
You are sunshine, you are shadows,
    you are morning and you are light.
You are hard times, you are good times, you are darkness and night.
I never wanted to give a man the things I want to give you.
I never wanted to live with a man the way I want to live with you.
You have brought me beautiful gifts,
gifts of life;
you have brought me love,
you have given me you.

GROOM

Yesterday there were gray clouds without light, but then there was a flame within me that began to grow. It was you, Cathy. I was a lonely man without a tomorrow, but your presence has brought peace to my heart. Together we found time to talk, to laugh, to cry, to love, to touch, and to care. Our music was the song of life. Live it, love it, love each other. Together we have discovered each other and ourselves.

We have found with each other a gift, a new life. We have found love and our love is alive and precious. And for tomorrow, I am filled with hope. There is a life worth living, a dream, a song to sing. Let's celebrate the gift of love. I hope we will continue to stand together, you and I, on top of the mountain, looking forward to each day with adventure, learning, and love. The gift I give you today is the promise to love you, Cathy, and to love you, and to love you.

Ritual: Bread and libation

CELEBRANT

Let us pause, break bread together, and drink so that we may dwell in this happy moment and remember this moment in the future. (*The celebrant passes the bread and libation; music is played.*)

Vows and double ring ceremony

CELEBRANT

Cathy, what do you promise Bob?

BRIDE

Bob, I promise to love you and to be your wife.

Let this ring I give you be a symbol of my promise, and let it also remind you of our past memories, our present happiness, and our future hope.

CELEBRANT

Bob, what do you promise Cathy?

GROOM

Cathy, I promise to love you and to be your husband.

Let this ring I give you be a symbol of my promise, and let it also remind you of our past memories, our present happiness, and our future hope.

Closing ritual: Toast, kiss, and recessional

BEST MAN or MAID OF HONOR (*pours libation and toasts the couple*)
On behalf of all who are here today and all who are friends of this radiant couple, I drink to long life and happiness for Bob and Cathy. The years of our lives are as a sacred cup poured out for us to drink. May the cup of your lives, Bob and Cathy, be sweet and full.

Drink now to each other from this bowl and so consecrate your marriage.

The bride and groom toast, then kiss, and the wedding closes with music and a recessional.

ॐ ॐ ॐ

A FATHER'S DAY WEDDING

This couple enjoyed very close relationships with their parents. They acknowledge their parents in this wedding, which took place on Father's Day.

ॐॐॐॐॐ

Opening

We hear a recorded version of "Our Love is Here to Stay." The celebrant and attendants are in place. The bride and groom come in together, arm in arm.

CELEBRANT

Let us make a wedding! Let us all join in love to celebrate the love of Jasmin and Brian. Let us share with them this moment when the relationship they have been creating moves to the new level of commitment called marriage.

BRIDE

Brian and I are delighted that you came to share in this memorable and happy occasion. To us, our wedding is a personal time of joy that we want to share with you. This is a beautiful day; enjoy it, and remember how good it is to be in love.

Acknowledgment of parents

GROOM

Each of you has touched our lives in some important way. As I have been contemplating marriage, my mother and father, the two people who have most shaped and influenced my life, have been present in my thoughts. I see them now as I never have before. They made a lifelong commitment to each other, as well as to their children, and while we've not always made it easy for them, they stuck to their commitment anyway. That has inspired me to be a better man. That is why I now would like to take this opportunity—on Father's Day—to say to them: Thank you, Mom and Dad. I love you.

BRIDE

On this Father's Day, I too, want to say to my parents: Thank you. I love you. You have helped teach me what a good relationship is all about. Through your strong commitment, you have learned to love each other and give as much as necessary to make your relationship work. From you I have learned that the most substantial and solid basis of a relationship is a sincere understanding of each other, an acceptance of one another's strengths and frailties, and the commitment to continually work at keeping communication open and loving. Thank you, Mom and Dad, for preparing me so well for this new adventure I am about to embark upon.

Celebrant's address

CELEBRANT

Our laws and customs require that we publicly acknowledge this new legal union, but Jasmin and Brian need neither ceremony nor process of law to tell them what they already know. This marriage does not begin today. It began when the two of them first decided to combine their separate lives into one. No one, neither the state, nor a religion, nor I can create this marriage. Only Brian and Jasmin can do that. This ceremony merely marks the moment when the relationship they have been creating moves to a new, richer meaning for each of them.

Jasmin and Brian, treat yourselves and each other with respect, and remind yourselves often of what brought you together. Take responsibility for making one another feel safe, and give the highest priority to the tenderness, gentleness, and kindness that your beloved deserves. When frustration, difficulty and fear assail your relationship, as they threaten all relationships at some time or another, remember to focus on what is *right* between you. In this way, you will ride out the times when clouds drift across the face of the sun; just because you may lose sight of it for a moment doesn't mean the sun has gone away.

We are ready now to mark the moment when this joyous affirmation is taken by Brian and Jasmin. Let us all be together, in this beautiful place, breathing the air that connects each of us with every other living thing. Let us be silent together, and consider the joy and courage that this man and this woman are demonstrating today. (*Silence.*)

Brian and Jasmin, I ask you now to affirm to each other that you freely choose to combine your lives in marriage.

Vows and Ring Ceremony

GROOM

Jasmin, I come to you today, complete in spirit, mind, and body, joyously alive and confident, to tell you what I truly feel: I want to be your husband. I want to grow beside you for the rest of my life, to smile or shed tears, to laugh or sigh, to be with you in all our changing selves. We have the thread of love weaving in and out of our experience. Let us follow that through the fabric of our life together.

BRIDE

To you, Brian, I promise to support you in all things that will help us grow. I will be honest and keep faith with you in all ways: in my mind, my heart, and my body. I promise to listen to you and to speak to you with understanding and patience. I will make it a daily commitment to see you as the independent person I love. I will open my heart, my eyes, and my mind to you. I will make every effort to continue growing. I will work with you to make our love ever more complete, more open, more intense, and more generous. I give you this ring as a token of my love.

GROOM

Jasmin, I want to walk beside you on this journey through life, whether uphill or down. I want to grow with you always and treat each day as a new adventure for us to experience together. And so, with this ring, I thee wed.

Blessing, pronouncement and kiss

CELEBRANT

May the steps you have just taken toward each other help you find new strength. May you find comfort, security, and vitality with each other. I call on all of you present to witness that Jasmin and Brian, having exchanged their promises, are now husband and wife, according to the laws of the State of Minnesota. Brian and Jasmin, you may now kiss.

Closing music: "Always."

ॐ ॐ ॐ

Guest Participation

A CANDLE-LIGHTING CEREMONY

Each guest in this ceremony participates in a ritual intended to evoke a sense of closeness and sharing, bringing their small group together, and introducing them to each other.

ॐॐॐॐॐ

Opening

CELEBRANT

Welcome, friends. Donna and Walter have invited us to join them today in their joy as they celebrate their union in marriage. Their commitment is not a new one, so this celebration does not mark a departure from their present relationship of mutual love. Rather, it reaffirms and strengthens this existing bond and declares it joyfully to the world.

Candle lighting ritual with guest participation and statements of appreciation

CELEBRANT

Because all of you who have come to celebrate this occasion are close to Donna and Walter, they would like each of you to participate, rather than merely witness their union. To make their recognition of each of you individually as someone loved by them, they will call you in turn by name. As they do, they would like you to come up here and light one small candle with the candle they will hand you. The many flames starting in this way from one original pair will symbolize the way Donna and Walter hope their love will heighten and enhance feelings of warmth and affection for all.

Donna and Walter light two large candles. Taking turns, each calls a guest's name. Using the large candles, each guest lights a small candle until everyone has lit one.

BRIDE *(lighting a candle)*
My beloved,

I love you freely without restrictions.

I love you honestly without deceit.

I love you now without reservations.

I love you physically without pretending.

I love you.

GROOM *(lighting a candle)*
My beloved,

May our joys be free of guilt,

And our sorrows free of regret.

May our open arms of love always

hold out the open hands of trust.

This I wish for you and me for all

our days on this earth.

Readings

FRIEND 1 (from *Blessed is the Light,* Grace Schulman)
*Blessed is the light that turns to fire, and blessed the flames
    that fire makes of what it burns.*

*Blessed the inexhaustible sun, for it feeds the moon that shines
    but does not burn.*

*Praised be hot vapors in earth's crust, for they force up
    mountains that explode as molten rock and cool, like
    love remembered.*

*Holy is the sun that strikes sea, for surely as water burns
    life and death are one....*

*Praised be the body, our bodies, that lie down and open and rise,
    falling in flame.*

FRIEND 2 (*Sudden Light,* Dante Gabriel Rossetti)
I have been here before,
But when or how I cannot tell:
I know the grass beyond the door,
The sweet keen smell,
The sighing sound, the lights around the shore.

You have been mine before,
How long ago I may not know
But just when at that swallow's soar
Your neck turned so,
Some veil did fall—I knew it all of yore.
Has this been thus before?
And shall not thus time's eddying flight
Still with our lives our love restore
In death's despite,
And day and night yield one delight once more?

Vows and ring ceremony

BRIDE (*places ring on groom's finger*)
Walter, accept this ring as a symbol of my love and as a sign that I
take you as my husband, to love, cherish, and grow with through all
of our days on this earth.

GROOM (*places ring on bride's finger*)
Donna, accept this ring as a symbol of my love and as a sign that I
take you as my wife, to love, cherish, and grow with through all of
our days on this earth.

Closing and kiss

CELEBRANT
Donna and Walter,
Take time with each other.
Let the seed of love grow and flourish with the seasons;
Spring's awareness
Summer's warmth
Autumn's understanding
Winter's serenity.

Bride and groom kiss

BRIDE AND GROOM

Come and join us in our celebration.

ॐ ॐ ॐ

Modern Ceremonies with a Traditional Tone

It is possible to shape a wedding ceremony so that it retains a formal, established and conventional resonance, yet allows a couple to express contemporary content within a traditional structure.

ॐॐॐॐॐ

A Unitarian Wedding

Opening Words

CELEBRANT

We are here in the name of that love which upholds and hallows the world. We gather in this place to honor the traditions of our forebears; we remember here the companionship of countless lovers in history. We are here in this place, in this hour, to declare before you who are assembled the love of Jonathan and Lisa, who come to this moment in freedom, with both vision and wisdom.

Question of Intent

CELEBRANT

Jonathan, do you come before this gathering of friends and family to proclaim your love and devotion for Lisa? Do you promise to affirm her and care for her during times of both joy and hardship? Forsaking all others, do you promise to be faithful to her, as long as you both shall live?

GROOM

I do.

CELEBRANT
> Lisa, do you come before this gathering of friends and family to proclaim your love and devotion for Jonathan? Do you promise to affirm him and care for him during times of both joy and hardship? Forsaking all others, do you promise to be faithful to him, as long as you both shall live?

BRIDE
> I do.

Reading

FRIEND (from *Fidelity*, D.H. Lawrence)
> *Man and woman are like the earth, that brings forth flowers*
> *in summer, and love, but underneath is rock.*
> *Older than flowers, older than ferns, older than* foraminiferae,
> *older than plasm altogether is the soul underneath.*
>
> *And when, throughout all the wild chaos of love*
> *slowly a gem forms, in the ancient, once-more-molten rocks*
> *of two human hearts, two ancient rocks, a man's heart and a woman's,*
> *that is the crystal of peace, the slow hard jewel of trust,*
> *the sapphire of fidelity.*
> *The gem of mutual peace emerging from the wild chaos of love.*

Blessing by the bride's family

CELEBRANT
> Do you, who have known Lisa for many years, and have seen her through times of joy and sorrow, now give blessing to her union with Jonathan?

BRIDE'S FAMILY
> We do!

Blessing by the groom's children

CELEBRANT

Joe and Melissa, you will share in this union, because your lives will inevitably be touched by the covenant which your father enters into today, and your participation will be needed to develop the bonds of a new family. As Jonathan and Lisa exchange their pledges in holy union, we ask from you also a pledge, that you will make room in your lives for Lisa, that you will join together with her to weave a fabric of help and comfort, and that you will help create a home in which all of you can grow to be the best people you can be. In this spirit, do you recognize and honor your new relationship with Lisa?

CHILDREN

We do.

Interlude: Spoken, silent, music, or prayer

Ritual: Wine, candle, or flower ceremony

Vows

CELEBRANT

Jonathan, will you have Lisa to be your beloved wife, to share your life with her, and do you pledge that you will love, honor and tenderly care for her, in ease and adversity, and do you promise never to close your heart against her?

GROOM

I do.

CELEBRANT

Lisa, will you have Jonathan to be your beloved husband, to share your life with him, and do you pledge that you will love, honor, and tenderly care for him, in ease and adversity, and do you promise never to close your heart against him?

BRIDE

I do.

Rings

GROOM

This ring I give you in token and pledge of my constant faith and abiding love.

BRIDE

This ring I give you in token and pledge of my constant faith and abiding love.

Closing: Pronouncement, embrace, benediction

CELEBRANT

Inasmuch as Jonathan and Lisa have declared their love before us and named their commitment aloud, we may all henceforth know that they are duly wed, united in the presence of the One who is love, eternal and compelling. What Spirit has blessed, let not the letter destroy; and let us all honor these two people with encouragement and support.

CELEBRANT *(to the couple)*

I invite you to signify your newly enhanced relationship with an embrace.

CELEBRANT

We celebrate the love that has brought you to this moment. With joy that deepens through many years, may you know its meaning and its mystery.

May your home be a place of happiness for all who enter it, a place where old and young are renewed in each other's company, a place for growing, a place for music and laughter.

And when shadows and darkness fall within its rooms, may it still be a place of hope and strength for you and for those who are entrusted to your care.

May no person be a stranger to your compassion, and may your larger family be the family of all humankind. And may those who are nearest to you and dearest to you be constantly enriched by the beauty and bounty of your love for one another.

Amen.

ॐ ॐ ॐ

A MEDIEVAL EXTRAVAGANZA

A spectacular, theatrical ceremony can reflect the dramatic, life-altering significance of a wedding. When a couple is able to lavish time, attention, and imagination in creating their ceremony, the outcome may be as striking and impressive as this example. Held in a grove of giant redwoods, this ceremony was written as a stage play, and has a large cast of characters. Costumes and decorations featured touches from the Middle Ages: large and colorful banners, feathered hats, brocaded dresses, and a wedding cake in the shape of a castle. The celebrant acted as master of ceremonies. The resulting joyful fantasy retains the formal essence of traditional nuptials.

Cast of characters

> The Bride
> The Groom
> Father of the Bride
> Mother of the Bride
> Mother of the Groom
> The Best Man
> The Maid of Honor
> The Bridesmaid
> The Herald
> A Musician
> The Singers
> The Gift Givers
> The Celebrant
> The Bird Holder
> The Trumpeter

Opening

A fanfare is heard from a trumpet inside the grove. The Herald walks out some distance from the entrance of the grove and speaks:

HERALD

Dear friends and relatives of Dana and Jimmy, the time has come to begin a ceremony of great joy and promise. Will you please follow me into this ring of trees and gather around me there!

The guests gather behind the Herald and proceed into the grove. The Herald arranges them in a semicircle facing south with the entrance on their right. The parents of the Bride and Groom enter the grove and stand facing the guests. The Celebrant enters the grove and stands in the center between the parents. The Singers begin singing "The Wedding Song." The Groom and Best Man enter the grove, followed after a few moments by the Bride's Attendants, the Maid of Honor, and the Bride.

Celebrant's address

CELEBRANT

Dear Dana and Jimmy. Today you are surrounded by your friends and family, all of whom are gathered to witness your marriage and to share in the joy of this occasion. Life has no single meaning so much as it is composed of many meaningful events, some of which can be specified and planned. One of these events is marriage.

As you know, no minister, no priest, no rabbi, no public official, can marry you. Only you can marry yourselves. By a mutual commitment to love each other, to work toward creating an atmosphere of care and consideration and respect, and by a willingness to face the tensions and anxieties that are a part of human life, you can make your wedded life come alive.

On this day of your marriage, you stand within the charmed circle of your love. But love is not meant to be the possession of two people alone. Rather it should serve as a source of common energy, as a form in which you find the strength to live your lives with courage. From this day onward, you have the opportunity to come closer together than ever before, and at the same time your love can allow you the strength to stand apart, to seek out your unique destinies, to make your special contribution to the world. You, together and individually, will create the meaning of your lives.

You will choose the values you will live by. If your love is honest and vital, it will make the choosing and living easier for you.

I should like to speak now of some of the things which we wish for you: We wish for you a love which makes both of you better people, which continues to give you joy and zest for living, which provides you with energy to face the responsibilities of life. We wish for you a home, an island of serenity and happiness, a place for beginning new efforts, a source of memories. May all that is noble, lovely, and true abide with you forever.

Welcome by the families

Dan and Norma, you are Dana's parents. Do you bestow upon Dana and Jimmy your good will, and pledge them your love and affection?

BRIDE'S PARENTS

Yes, we do, and we welcome Jimmy into our family.

CELEBRANT

Joan, you are Jimmy's mother. Do you bestow upon Dana and Jimmy your good will, and pledge them your love and affection?

GROOM'S MOTHER

Yes, I do, and I welcome Dana into my family.

Contributions by friends

CELEBRANT

Stuart and Sandi, you have a gift of song for your friends, Jimmy and Dana.

THE SINGERS

Stuart and Sandi sing the song "'Twas a Lover and His Lass."

CELEBRANT

Bill, you have been a friend of Dana and Jimmy. What do you wish for them?

GIFT GIVER 1

We are engaged in a unique ceremony. While all nature's creatures choose partners, few of these relationships are lasting. What makes men and women special is love, the quality that sets us apart from other living things. Love is what makes us human.

Dana and Jimmy, I wish you love. I wish you love everlasting. I wish you love fulfilling. I wish you love's peace and love's pleasure. But most of all, I wish you love's friendship.

CELEBRANT
Martha, what will you say to your friends Dana and Jimmy?

GIFT GIVER 2 (from *Give All to Love*, Ralph Waldo Emerson)
Give all to love;
Obey thy heart;
Friends, kindred, days,
Estate, good fame,
Plans, credit and the Muse—
Nothing refuse.

'Tis a brave master;
Let it have scope:
Follow it utterly,
Hope beyond hope:
High and more high
It dives into noon,
With wing unspent,
Untold intent;
But it is a god,
Knows its own path
And the outlets of the sky.

It was never for the mean;
It requireth courage stout,
Souls above doubt,
Valour unbending,
Such 'twill reward;—
They shall return
More than they were,
And ever ascending....

Vows

The musicians play "Let It Be Me." The Bride and Groom move to stand side by side facing the guests.

GROOM

Dana, I stand here today to join my life with yours as your husband. I do this because I believe that although the music of a single instrument may be beautiful, the music of two instruments played together may be far more beautiful, for the sound of each influences the sound of the other. So it is for me, that with you I am capable of feelings, efforts, and accomplishments that I could not have alone. We are able to perform together a duet of great enjoyment and satisfaction to me, in exquisite and exciting harmony, sharing the leadership of our song. Few of the notes we will play tomorrow are known to us today. It is our skill as musicians that keeps the song alive. So long as there is music in me, I will play with you as my partner.

BRIDE

Jimmy, I have chosen you above all others to be my life partner. You are special to me in many different ways. You are my best friend. I can go to you with all my joys and sorrows. You are my playmate. I love to tickle you and run with you. You are my lover. Your gaze and touch excite me. I know that honesty is paramount in our relationship, and I pledge that it will always be so. I promise always to give you space and support you in all endeavors. I love you, Jimmy. I want you to be my husband.

Grow old along with me!
The best is yet to be,
The last of life, for which the first was made.[11]

Ring ceremony

The Maid of Honor takes the bouquet from the Bride and hands her the Groom's ring.

BRIDE (*places the ring on the Groom's finger and says*)
Jimmy, I give you this ring as a gift of love and as a symbol of our commitment.

The Best Man hands the Groom the Bride's ring.

GROOM (*places the ring on the Bride's finger and says*)
Dana, I give you this ring as a gift of love and as a symbol of our

commitment.

Wine ritual

The Maid of Honor takes a bottle of wine from a basket. She hands the bottle to the Bride. The Best Man takes a wine glass from the basket and hands it to the Groom. The Bride pours some wine into the Groom's glass. Then she hands him the wine bottle. Meanwhile, the Maid of Honor has taken another wine glass from the basket. Now, she hands the wine glass to the Bride. The Groom pours some wine into the Bride's glass and then hands the wine bottle back to the Maid of Honor, who puts it back in the basket.

BEST MAN

Let this drinking of wine remind you that what matters most in life is the spirit, not the letter. The future is forever in the making, so do not cling too long to the present, however satisfying, lest it become an anchor and therefore a dead past, rather than a springboard and therefore a vital past. (*Bride and Groom drink the wine.*)

BEST MAN

May your days and years to come be filled with love and joy. And if your affection for each other always has a little more to grow, it will rise from you and enter the lives of others, enriching and strengthening them. As Saint-Exupéry puts it, "Love does not consist in gazing into each other's eyes, but in looking in the same direction." [12]

Groom hands his wine glass to the Best Man. Bride hands hers to the Maid of Honor. The wine glasses are returned to the basket.

Closing with pronouncement, release of doves, kiss and recessional

CELEBRANT

Dana and Jimmy—in expressing your private affirmations before this public company, you have pronounced yourselves husband and wife.

The Bird Holder releases the birds, which fly out of the grove.

Like these birds, flying on their separate paths, you will travel your separate ways together, always being each other's best friend.

Bride and Groom kiss. The Trumpeter plays a joyous fanfare. The wedding party goes to greet the guests.

ॐ ॐ ॐ

A Classical, Literary Pageant

This couple shares deeply held values concerning the importance of freedom, honesty, and courage in their relationship. This ceremony proclaims their beliefs. It was printed on elegant paper and rolled into scrolls as mementos for each guest.

ॐॐॐॐॐ

The couple shall face south, the man on the woman's right. The celebrant shall begin by saying:

We stand where Nature's conflicts are resolved;

Here the heights stand poised beside the plains;

Here daylight melts into awaiting night;

The City of the Known lies below us,

The tracks of knowledge yet to come, above;

It is fitting, in this place of union,

To celebrate the union that is Love,

As these two here before us have affirmed it.

Then addressing the couple, the celebrant shall say:

Charles and Letitia,

We cannot be if we are not brave

We will not be if we are not honest,

And we should not be if we are not free;

Your liberty, your candor, and your courage,

These three things are what have brought you here,

And these it is that you have come to pledge.

Then the celebrant, calling the man by his name, shall say:

Charles, will you have this woman as your wife:

She brings to you her love;

She brings it with courage,

She brings it without deceit or reservation,

And she brings it freely.

The man shall answer:

I do.

Then the celebrant, calling the woman by her name, shall say:

Letitia, will you have this man as your husband:

He brings to you his love;

He brings it with courage,

He brings it without deceit or reservation,

And he brings it freely.

The woman shall answer:

I do.

Then the celebrant shall say:

Who gives this woman to be married?

The friend of the bride shall then answer:

No one gives her; no one can.

She gives herself.

The man shall then, using his right hand, take the woman by her right hand and say:

I, Charles, take thee, Letitia, to be my lawful, wedded wife;

may we together cast a single lot,

and doing so, may our fate find in us

a fitting channel for the stream of life.

The woman shall then take the man by his right hand and say likewise:

I, Letitia, take thee, Charles, to be my lawful wedded husband;

may we together cast a single lot,

and doing so, may our fate find in us

a fitting channel for the stream of life.

The celebrant shall give the man a ring; he shall place it upon the ring finger of the woman's left hand, saying:

This ring shall be symbol of what we two pursue together;

a part and yet a whole,

divided but indivisible;

without beginning and without end.

Then the celebrant shall say to all present:

By the authority committed to me, I declare that Charles and Letitia are now husband and wife, according to their own agreement and the laws of the State of Colorado.

The celebrant then offers a blessing:

We know not what the future may bring into the life of this couple, but we pray that together they may be equal to the needs of their tomorrows. May they find patience in time of stress, strength in time of weakness, courage in time of discouragement, vision in time of doubt, and, in all times, a growing love.

ॐ ॐ ॐ

Minimal Ceremonies

The celebrant marries the couple

CELEBRANT
Do you, Elaine, take George to be your husband?

BRIDE
I do.

CELEBRANT
Do you, George, take Elaine to be your wife?

GROOM
I do.

CELEBRANT
I then pronounce you husband and wife.

ॐॐॐॐॐ

The couple marries themselves

GROOM
I, Daniel, take you, Rochelle, to be my wife. Let this ring be a symbol of my vow.

BRIDE
I, Rochelle, take you, Daniel to be my husband. Let this ring be a symbol of my vow.

CELEBRANT
Insomuch as you have exchanged your vows of marriage, I now pronounce that you are husband and wife.

ॐॐॐॐॐ

To keep your marriage brimming,
with love in the wedding cup,
whenever you're wrong, admit it;
whenever you're right, shut up.
—Ogden Nash

Chapter 16

Dealing with Stage Fright

The only thing we have to fear is fear itself.
—F. D. Roosevelt

Don't let stage fright prevent you from taking an active part in—and enjoying—your wedding ceremony. Almost everyone feels some tension when they perform in public; it's a normal and expected part of public speaking. Even accomplished actors often experience clammy hands, a racing heart, fluttery stomach, or dry mouth in anticipation of a public appearance.

Unfortunately, for many, that anxiety can become so intense that it interferes with their ability to function. At its worst, it feels something like this: *My heart starts beating so fast that it feels like it's going to explode. My throat closes and I can't breathe so I start to choke. My hands start sweating and I have to hold on to keep from falling. I know I'm going to die. I want to run, but I don't know where.*

These fears come from irrational thoughts. We're afraid we might appear foolish or stupid, and we become embarrassed because we're being watched.

To conquer fear of public speaking, you need to gain control of your body, your mind, and your feelings. Fortunately, there are effective stress management strategies for controlling and reducing nervousness. With practice, you can learn to release soothing, calming biochemicals instead of those that activate tension and anxiety.

ॐ ॐ ॐ

Stress Reduction Exercises

First, create a positive mental attitude. Keep in mind that your wedding ceremony is not an appearance before a jury. Your guests are on your side—they are your family and friends; they are rooting for you. They know that you are not a professional actor. Remember that a wedding ceremony enjoys so much goodwill that nothing can really go wrong.

Second, don't be afraid that your emotions will overwhelm you. Your wedding *is* a highly emotional event. If you feel teary, it's okay; if the words don't come out easily, it's okay. Everyone will be moved by, and sympathetic to, your strong feelings. Just pause for a moment, breathe, and let that intense moment pass, then continue. Everyone will understand.

Third, if you use techniques of slow breathing, relaxation, and positive self-talk and imagery, you will increase your comfort and confidence while you're on view, getting married.

ॐॐॐॐॐ

A few days before the ceremony find a comfortable place where you will not be disturbed. Breathe deeply and let your breath out slowly while gently telling yourself to "let go and relax." Then imagine the ceremony, step by step, *as you want it to happen.* See yourself being confident and relaxed. Imagine it in detail. Rehearse it in your mind—how you will walk, how you and your partner will stand, who will say what, how pleased your guests will be. Then, go through the ceremony again. Mentally preparing yourself in this way will make the actual event feel familiar, and therefore less anxiety provoking. Repeat this process several times before the actual ceremony.

To relax your body, use the following exercise several times during the few days before your wedding:

1. Take a long, slow, deep breath.
2. Beginning with your toes, tighten each muscle group as much as possible, hold for a moment, then, all at once, let go and take another long slow breath.
3. Then slowly do the same with legs, abdomen, upper torso, and your back. Again, take a long, slow, deep breath.
4   Then move on to shoulders, arms, and hands. Tighten, hold, then let go. Breathe deeply.
5. Finally, tighten the muscles of your neck, face, and scalp in the same manner.
6. If you still sense any remaining physical tension, focus on the tense part of your body and repeat this contract, hold, release and breathe process until you feel comfortably relaxed.
7. Just before the ceremony begins, while you are waiting, take a deep breath, let it out slowly, and remind yourself that you know how to relax your body and calm your mind. Remember that this is a joyous occasion and allow yourself to feel relaxed and confident.
8. As you walk to your place, breathe deeply, stand tall, and feel your confidence and a sense of well-being.
9. When you're in place, take another deep breath, and let it out slowly. Remind yourself again to relax. Keep your knees unlocked and slightly bent, and let your shoulders drop and hang loosely. Focus all your attention on your spouse-to-be, the celebrant, and the words that are being said.
10. Just before you begin to speak, take still another deep breath, let it out slowly, and smile. Remember that you can pause at any time to breathe deeply and relax. Such a pause will seem natural to your guests. Take a slow, deep breath whenever you begin to feel anxious.

ꙅꙅꙅꙅꙅ

Relaxation is a learned response. Even very anxious people can learn to reduce their anxiety using these exercises. Give yourself time to repeat them until you feel your body let go.

Fear is always based on worries about the future, so live in each moment and don't let your imagination run wild. Maintain a cheerful and optimistic attitude and enjoy your wedding!

ꙅꙅꙅꙅꙅ

Nothing in life is to be feared.
It is only to be understood.

—Marie Curie

Chapter 17

Resources and References

Where there is great love
there are always miracles.
—Willa Cather

Finding a Cooperative Celebrant

There are several religious organizations that encourage couples to develop personal wedding ceremonies. These are groups that emphasize individual responsibility and personal choice. Listed below are the national offices of several of these liberal religious organizations.

American Humanist Association
Division of Humanist Counseling
7 Harwood Drive
Amherst, NY 14226

American Ethical Union
2 West 64th Street
New York, NY 10023

Unitarian-Universalist Association
25 Beacon Street
Boston, MA 02108

Universal Life Church
601 Third Street
Modesto, CA 95351

Metropolitan Community Churches
8714 Santa Monica Boulevard
West Hollywood, CA 90069

ぇぇぇぇぇ

If you want a religious ceremony, liberal churches and liberal clergy within traditional churches may permit you to participate in developing your wedding ceremony. Ministers, priests, and rabbis often are willing to incorporate your ideas into traditional ceremonies. You can check the following resources.

- Contact your own clergy.
- Look in the Yellow Pages under *Churches* (alternative, community, humanist, interdenominational, New Age, nondenominational, etc.).
- Look under wedding consultants or wedding chapels. Wedding consultants are especially likely to know about celebrants who will work with couples in nontraditional ways.
- Call the Council of Churches, the Council of Liberal Churches, or the Union of American Hebrew Congregations and ask for a referral to a liberal minister or rabbi.
- Call clergy involved in ministries near a college campus.
- Check the business personals under *Weddings* in your local newspaper.
- Check to see whether a judge or justice of the peace would be willing to help you create your own ceremony.
- Find a ship's captain and get married on board.

- Some communities or states have printed reference guides listing all types of wedding resources. In California, *Here Comes the Guide,* by Lynn Broadwell is an especially valuable resource.
- Check the Internet.
- Talk to friends for further leads.

శ్రీ శ్రీ శ్రీ

Suggested Readings

SUGGESTIONS FOR WEDDING POETRY AND READINGS

Hass, R. and S. Mitchell, editors. *Into the Garden: A Wedding Anthology.* New York: HarperCollins, 1993.

Munro, E., editor. *Wedding Readings: Centuries of Writing and Rituals for Love and Marriage.* New York: Viking, 1989.

Nikuradse, T. *African-American Wedding Readings.* New York: Dutton, 1998.

Rubenstein, H., editor. *Oxford Book of Marriage.* New York: Oxford University Press, 1990.

SUGGESTIONS FOR CONTEMPORARY WEDDING VOWS

Anastasio, J. and M. Bevilacqua. *The Everything Wedding Vows Book.* Holbrook, MA: Adams, 1994.

Elkof, B. *With These Words I Thee Wed: Contemporary Wedding Vows for Today's Couples.* Boston: Adams, 1989.

Glusker, D. and P. Misner. *Words For Your Wedding.* New York: Harper and Row, 1986.

Kingma, D. *Weddings From the Heart.* Berkeley, CA: Conari Press, 1991.

Rollin, B. *I Thee Wed.* New York: Doubleday, 1961.

Warner, D. *Complete Book of Wedding Vows.* Franklin Lakes, NJ: Career Press, 1996.

Suggestions for Wedding Customs and Traditions from Around the World

Leviton, R. *Weddings By Design: A Guide to the Non-Traditional Ceremony*. San Francisco: Harper, 1993.

Cole, H. *Jumping the Broom: The African-American Wedding Planner*. New York: Holt, 1993.

Costa, S. *Wild Geese and Tea: An Asian-American Wedding Planner,* New York: Riverhead Books, 1997.

Sturgis, I. *The Nubian Wedding Book: Words and Rituals to Celebrate and Plan an African-American Wedding*. New York: Three Rivers Press, 1997.

Suggestions for Updating Traditional Ceremonies

Brill, M., et al., editors. *Write Your Own Wedding: A Personal Guide for Couples of All Faiths*. Chicago: Follett, 1979.

Diamant, A. *The New Jewish Wedding*. New York: Summit Books, 1985.

Hawxhurst, Joan C. *Interfaith Wedding Ceremonies: Samples and Sources*. Kalamazoo, MI: Dovetail Publishing, 1996.

Packham, J. *Wedding Ceremonies: Planning Your Special Day*. New York: Sterling Publishing, 1993.

Suggestions for Managing Your Wedding

Broadwell, L. *Here Comes the Guide*. Berkeley, CA: Hopscotch Press, 1998.

Neel, Steven M. *Saying "I Do": The Wedding Ceremony, The Complete Guide to a Perfect Wedding*. Colorado Springs, CO: Meriwether Publishing Ltd, 1995.

Suggestions for Maintaining a Healthy Marriage

Gottman, John M., Ph.D. *The Seven Principles for Making Marriage Work*. New York: Crown Publishers, 1999.

Tannen, Deborah. *You Just Don't Understand: Men and Women in Conversation*. New York: Ballantine, 1991.

ॐ ॐ ॐ

Notes

Chapter 8

1. p. 79. From "On Marriage" in *The Prophet*, by Kahlil Gibran, New York: Alfred A. Knopf, 1923, renewed 1951.
2. p. 80–81. Joseph Campbell, source and publisher unknown.

Chapter 9

3. p. 96. See Richard Leviton, *Weddings by Design: A Guide to the Non-Traditional Ceremony*, San Francisco, Harper, 1993.
4. p. 98–99. Adapted from *Diane Warner's Complete Book of Wedding Vows*. See also Richard Leviton, *Weddings by Design*.
5. p. 100–101. For a more traditional version of this ritual, see Richard Leviton, *Weddings by Design*.

Chapter 12

6. p. 131. Found in *Wedding Readings: Centuries of Writing and Rituals for Love and Marriage,* edited by E. Munro, New York, Viking, 1989.
7. p. 134. Found in *Wedding Readings,* (no source given) edited by E. Munro, New York, Viking, 1989.
8. p. 142–143. Found in *Interfaith Wedding Ceremonies: Samples and Sources,* edited by Joan C. Hauxhurst, Kalamazoo, Mich., Dovetail Publishing, 1996.

Chapter 15

9. p. 162. Jalal al-din Rumi, title and publisher unknown.
10. p. 170. From a story by A. C. Banson found in *Wedding Readings,* edited by E. Munro, New York, Viking, 1989.
11. p. 192. Robert Browning, from "Rabbi Ben Ezra."
12. p. 193. Antoine de Saint-Exupéry, from *The Little Prince*.

Index

Permissions

Grateful acknowledgment is given for permission to use the following:

Excerpts from Song of Songs. Scripture quotations are taken from the *Good News Bible in Today's English Version,* Second Edition. Copyright © 1992 by American Bible Society. Used by permission.

Excerpt from "Poetry and Marriage: The Use of Old Forms" from *Standing by Words* by Wendell Berry. Copyright © 1983 by Wendell Berry. Reprinted by permission of North Point Press, a division of Farrar, Straus & Giroux, Inc.

"love is more thicker than forget," copyright 1939, © 1967, 1991 by the Trustees for the E. E. Cummings Trust, from *Complete Poems: 1904-1962* by E. E. Cummings, edited by George J. Firmage. Reprinted by permission of Liveright Publishing Corporation.

"Love Song" by Gloria Elizabeth. Copyright © 1973 by Gloria (Broman) Elizabeth. Used by permission of the author.

"Of the First Kiss" from *The Voice of the Master* by Kahlil Gibran. Copyright © 1958, 1986 by Anthony R. Ferris. Published by arrangement with Carol Publishing Group. A Citadel Press Book.

"Love in the Middle of the Air," from *Word Alchemy* by Lenore Kandel. Copyright © 1967 by Lenore Kandel. Used by permission of Grove/Atlantic, Inc.

"Fidelity" by D. H. Lawrence, from *The Complete Poems of D. H. Lawrence* by D. H. Lawrence, edited by V. de Sola Pinto and F. W. Roberts. Copyright © 1964, 1971 by Angelo Ravagli and C. M. Weekley, Executors of the Estate of Frieda Lawrence Ravagli. Used by permission of Viking Penguin, a division of Penguin Putnam Inc.

"The Wife" by Denise Levertov, from *Collected Earlier Poems 1940–1960.* Copyright © 1949, 1979 by Denise Levertov. Reprinted by permission of New Directions Publishing Corp.

Quote from *Gift From the Sea* by Anne Morrow Lindbergh. Copyright © 1955, 1975, renewed 1983 by Anne Morrow Lindbergh. Reprinted by permission of Pantheon Books, a division of Random House, Inc.

Psalm I translated by Stephen Mitchell from *The Enlightened Heart: An Anthology of Sacred Poetry,* edited by Stephen Mitchell. Copyright © 1989 by Stephen Mitchell. Adapted by Stephen Mitchell in *Into the Garden: A Wedding Anthology,* edited by Robert Hass and Stephen Mitchell. Copyright © 1993 by Robert Hass and Stephen Mitchell. Reprinted by permission of HarperCollins Publishers, Inc.

Psalm 100 translated and adapted by Stephen Mitchell from *Into the Garden: A Wedding Anthology,* edited by Robert Hass and Stephen Mitchell. Copyright © 1993 by Robert Hass and Stephen Mitchell. Reprinted by permission of HarperCollins Publishers, Inc.

Excerpts from *Letters* by Rainer Maria Rilke, and *The Imitation of Christ* by Thomas à Kempis translated by Stephen Mitchell, from *Into the Garden: A Wedding Anthology,* edited by Robert Hass and Stephen Mitchell. Copyright © 1993 by Robert Hass and Stephen Mitchel. Reprinted by permission of HarperCollins Publishers, Inc.

Excerpt from *Letters to a Young Poet* by Rainer Maria Rilke, translated by Stephen Mitchell. Copyright © 1984 by Stephen Mitchell. Reprinted by permission of Random House, Inc.

Quote from *Notes on Love and Courage* by Hugh Prather. Copyright © 1977 by Hugh Prather. Used by permission of Doubleday, a division of Random House, Inc.

"The Minute I Heard My First Love Story" by Jalal al-din Rumi, translated by John Moynes and Coleman Barks. Copyright © 1984. Originally published in *Open Secret: Versions of Rumi* by Threshold Books, 139 Main Street, Brattleboro, VT 05301. Used by permission.

"Persian Love Poem," from *Mystical Poems of Rumi,* translated by A. J. Arberry. Copyright © 1968 by A. J. Arberry. All rights reserved. Reprinted by permission of University of Chicago Press.

Excerpt from "Blessed is the Light" by Grace Schulman. From *Hemispheres: Poems.* Copyright © 1984, 1995 by Grace Schulman. Used by permission of Sheep Meadow Press.

"The Greatest Gift" (adapted) by Katharine Whiteside Taylor in *Inward Light*, XXIX:69, Spring 1966. Copyright © 1966 by Katharine Whiteside Taylor. Used by permission of Margot Taylor Fanger, and Katharine Taylor Loesch.

Excerpt from "Oaths of Friendship" from *Translations from the Chinese* by Arthur Waley, trans. Copyright 1919 and renewed 1947 by Arthur Waley. Reprinted by permission of Alfred A. Knopf Inc.

"Seven Steps." Reprinted, with permission of the publisher, from *Diane Warner's Complete Book of Wedding Vows* © 1996 Diane Warner. Published by Career Press, Franklin Lakes, NJ.

"June 17, 1846, on the North Platte" from *Tamsen Donner: A Woman's Journey* by Ruth Whitman. Copyright © 1977 by Ruth Whitman. Published by alicejamesbooks, Cambridge, MA. Used by permission of the author.

"'Twixt You and Me" by Madam Kuan, translated by Lin Yutang, from *The Importance of Living* by Lin Yutang. Copyright © 1937, renewed 1965, by Lin Tai-yi and Hsiang Ju Lin. By permission of William Morrow & Co., Inc.

Every effort has been made to trace copyright holders, but in a few cases this has proved impossible. The publishers would be interested to hear from any copyright holders not acknowledged here, and will make corrections to any subsequent editions of this work.

Hail wedded love, mysterious law,
true source of all humanity.

—John Milton

To order additional copies of

Weddings
The Magic of Creating Your Own Ceremony

Book: $19.95   Shipping/Handling: $3.50

Contact: ***BookPartners, Inc.***
P.O. Box 922
Wilsonville, OR 97070

E-mail: bpbooks@teleport.com
Fax: 503-682-8684
Phone: 503-682-9821
Order: 1-800-895-7323